MW00902810

# Cooking For Life's Special Occasions

## Stephanie Bergsma

cookingforlifecookbook@gmail.com

www.cookingforlifecookbo.wix.com/cookingforlife

www.facebook.com/cookingforlifecookbook

Published December 2013

ISBN-13: 978-1493623471
ISBN-10:1493623478

# Table of Contents ................................. 2

**Dedication** ................................................7
**Author's Note** .........................................9
**About this book** ...................................11
**What is Gluten?** ..................................12
**Gluten Free Flours** ............................13
**5 Common Gluten Free Mistakes** ...........14
**Hidden Sources of Gluten** ................20
**Tips for Gluten Free Success** ...............22
**Where are you getting your Fibre?** ..........25
**Why Vegan/Vegetarian?** ..................30
**Tips to get you started on a Plant-based diet** ........33

# Menus and Recipes: ......................... 35

## Picnic in the Park ................................. 37
**Rosemary Corn Crackers** .........................40
**Curried Zucchini Hummus** .......................42
**Quiche** ................................................43
**Quinoa Tabbouleh** ...............................44
**Perfect Pie Crust** ...............................46
**Thumbprint Cookies** ..............................48

## Christmas Dinner .................................. 51
**Garlic Baked Squash** ...............................54
**Braised Peas** .........................................55

## Christmas Dinner Cont'd

Baked Rice Loaf .................................................. 56
Mashed Potatoes Supreme ................................. 57
Mushroom Gravy .............................................. 58
Cheesecake with Raspberry Sauce ...................... 60

## Happy Birthday! .......................................... 65

Creamy Pasta Bake ........................................... 68
Mini Pizzas ...................................................... 70
Pizza Sauce ..................................................... 72
Yogurt Yum-Yum Popsicles ................................ 73
Orange Delight Cupcakes .................................. 74
Cherry Fudgesicles or Ice Cream ........................ 76

## Thanksgiving .............................................. 79

Stamppot Carrots ............................................. 82
Roasted Root Vegetables ................................... 84
Sauteed Greens ................................................ 85
Green Bean Casserole ....................................... 86
Stuffing .......................................................... 88
Savory Baked Tofu ........................................... 90
Maple Pecan Tarts ............................................ 91

## Baby or Bridal Shower ................................. 95

Lettuce Wraps ................................................. 98
Eggless "Egg" Salad .......................................... 99
Chick Pea Tuna Salad ........................................ 100
Hummus .......................................................... 101
Zucchini Relish ................................................ 102
Summer Tomato Salad ....................................... 104
Lentil Salad ..................................................... 105
Curried Rice Salad ............................................ 106
Blueberry Cream Trifle ...................................... 108

# Backyard Barbecue ......................................... 113
Barbecue Sauce ....................................116
Potato Salad .......................................117
Salsa Skillet Pasta ................................118
Lemony Dill Pickles ...............................119
Black Bean Burgers ..............................120
Creamy Garlic Spread ...........................122
Avocado Key Lime Pie ..........................123

# Brunch ........................................................ 127
Blueberry Muffins (with variations) ..........130
Cranberry Banana Muffins ....................132
Oatmeal Raisin Scones.........................134
Fruit Kebabs ......................................136
Orange Strawberry Banana Smoothie......137
Banana Blueberry Pancakes ..................138

# Games Night................................................ 141
Potato Skins.......................................144
Pizza Popcorn ....................................146
Guacamole ........................................147
Hot Broccoli & Mushroom Dip................148
Mexican Pie .......................................150
Peppermint Patty Brownies ...................152

# Lunch with Friends......................................... 155
Cream of Cauliflower Soup....................158
Curried Pumpkin Soup..........................160
Veggie Taco Salad ..............................162
Multigrain Loaf ...................................164
Strawberry Macaroon Bars....................166

# Romantic Dinner For Two ........................... 169

Zesty Kale Salad ........................................ 172
Garlic Bread ............................................... 173
Veggie Pasta Sauce.................................... 174
Sweetheart Brownies for Two...................... 176

# Movie Night ................................................ 181

Mexican Chili Corn Pie .............................. 184
Cheeze Sauce ........................................... 186
Sunflower Sour Cream................................ 188
Banana Splits............................................. 189
Banana Coconut Ice Cream ...................... 190

# Seasonings and Extras ............................ 193

Parmesan Cheeze Please! ......................... 194
Curry Powder Substitute ............................ 195
Chicken-style Seasoning ........................... 196
Measuring Equivalents ............................... 197
List of beans.............................................. 198
Bean Cooking Chart .................................. 199
Dried bean quick-soak method .................. 200
Pantry Checklist......................................... 202
Resources ................................................. 206
Index ........................................................ 209

To Matthew, Ryan, Joel & Ella
You make every Special
Occasion one to remember.
xoxo

# Author's Note:

In almost every culture around the world, food is at the centre of most special occasions. The menu is carefully thought out and planned, ingredients are purchased and time is taken to prepare these foods that are such an integral part of our celebrations. Christmases at Grandma's house, birthday parties, summer barbecues and picnics in the park all have fond memories tied to them, not just because of the time spent with family and friends but also because of the special foods that have been prepared for just such an occasion. Usually the best of the best are reserved for these gatherings and if you're like me, it's almost more fun to make these special treats than it is to eat them! (almost!)

One of my favorite food memories is having a special German tradition of "riced potatoes" - cooked potatoes that have been put through a press and come out resembling rice. Thanksgiving and Christmas just weren't the same if these fluffy potatoes were not served! Even today when we have holiday meal at my parents' house, I insist on having riced potatoes because it "wouldn't be the same without them".

I hope you enjoy my second cookbook – it's been fun to design it in a "not-so-traditional" sort of way, organizing it by events and menus rather than by types of food. I hope you enjoy these foods as much as my family and I do!
Make sure to take the time to savor Life's Special Occasions!
God bless,

Stephanie

# About this book:

I'm very excited to introduce my second cookbook! My first cookbook, Cooking For Life – A Total Vegetarian, Wheat Free and Gluten Free Cooking Experience – was officially released in April of 2013. I've been busy these past few months trying to get out the book that is in your hands – Cooking For Life's Special Occasions. I wanted to lay it out in a different way than a traditional cookbook that usually has different categories grouping similar recipes together – i.e. Soups and Salads, Desserts, Main Courses, etc.

Instead of the traditional format, I decided to organize it by special occasions. This doesn't mean that you can only use the Christmas section for Christmas or the Picnic section for picnics! Oh no – quite the opposite! Please make the recipes your own and mix and match them to suit your needs. I hope that the format I chose will help you out with the various special occasions that will arise because I know how challenging it can be for someone with dietary restrictions to enjoy special functions without worrying about the menu. I hope this will allow you to host more functions and outings without having to wonder what you're going to serve.

All of the recipes are free from gluten (I have included wheat free oats, however, which are gluten free but can't be deemed that way in Canada) wheat, dairy, lactose, eggs, cholesterol and animal products. Every ingredient is easy to find as well.

I pray that this book will be a blessing to you and encourage you to enjoy Life's Special Occasions!

# What is Gluten?

- Gluten is a type of protein naturally found in wheat, rye, barley (also known as "malt") and their derivatives (including, but not limited to, spelt, kamut, couscous and bulgur)
- Gluten gives bread its chewy texture
- In Canada, oats are considered unsafe for those avoiding gluten – due to cross contamination. Other countries have their own definition of "gluten free" so it's best to check with your own country's food labelling/allergy laws
- Wheat free oats are readily available and are tested frequently to ensure safety
- Millet can be treated the same way as oats and should be cautiously consumed by anyone with a gluten allergy/sensitivity

# Gluten Free Flours

When it comes to gluten free flours, there isn't one that will replace gluten-containing flours perfectly by itself. Gluten free baking will yield much better results if a combination of flour is used. The texture will be closer to that of something baked with wheat flour and you won't have the overpowering taste that you would have if only one gluten free flour is used.

Below is a list of the most commonly used and readily available gluten free flours and starches on the market today.

- Almond flour
- Amaranth flour
- Arrowroot flour
- Bean flour
- Buckwheat flour
- Chick pea flour
- Coconut flour
- Cornstarch
- Millet flour*
- Oat flour*
- Potato starch
- Rice flour
- Sorghum flour
- Tapioca starch
- Teff flour

*Please note that although millet flour and oat flour both naturally contain no gluten, they are both very prone to cross-contamination in the cutting, harvesting and packaging process. Ensure that your product says gluten free (or in the case of oats in Canada – "Wheat Free") on the packaging.

# 5 Common Gluten Free Mistakes

When anyone is first advised to avoid gluten, for whatever reason, it can be overwhelming! With the internet age comes the overabundance of information – both reliable and not so reliable. One can quickly get "information-overload" and become overwhelmed and confused.

Many times, as well, doctors will refer their patients to dieticians or nutritionists and while individuals in these professions are both well-trained and informative, sometimes their understanding and information regarding gluten-free living is lacking. This is not saying anything about their training or education; it is usually due to the fact that they do not live with this restriction and therefore do not know every hidden word that translates into "gluten" on labels, which brands are more reliable than others, or simply how to successfully live day to day avoiding gluten in a gluten-saturated world.

There are 5 common mistakes that people often make regarding a gluten free lifestyle. I've outlined these in the next few pages and hopefully it will help you and your loved ones to understand gluten and gluten-free living much better!

# 1. Not understanding gluten

In a world where food allergies are on the rise, it's really challenging to keep up with what is in everything! It makes it especially hard when food companies use every word EXCEPT the allergen on their labels (i.e. *malt* instead of *barley* or *gluten*).

My mom has been on a wheat-free diet for many years, long before food allergy-awareness was something that anyone cared to talk about. My grandmother decided to make my mom a cake so she presented my mom with a Duncan Hines cake-mix cake. My mom had to inform my grandma that, although she appreciated the thought, she really couldn't eat it. My grandmother was surprised because she knew that my mom couldn't have "flour". Her response? "How can there be flour in it? I didn't add any!" She naturally assumed because she didn't add any that there couldn't possibly be any in the box because the label didn't clearly say "wheat flour".

I remember several years ago being in a hospital waiting room and picking up a cooking magazine to peruse while I waited. I turned to an article, written by a well-known chef, about the perfect way to roast a turkey. I decided to keep reading to see what his method was. He suggested putting potatoes in the roasting pan alongside the turkey. He said that cooking the potatoes this way would "release their gluten" and help to thicken the drippings better. I was astonished and upset all at the same time; astonished because I couldn't believe that a person who spends so much time around food could be so misinformed as to think that there was gluten in potatoes; upset because I thought of all the people besides me who had read or would read the same article and think that there is gluten in potatoes! Clearly, he must have meant "starch" but used the wrong word; however, this is just one example of how people can be easily confused as to what "gluten" really means.

## 2. Confusing "Gluten-Free" with "Wheat-Free"

When you see a product labelled "Wheat Free" – many people think that's synonymous with "Gluten Free"; after all, wheat has gluten in it right? Well, yes but that's not the entire story.

There are many things *besides* wheat that have gluten – including barley, rye, spelt, and kamut. And to make it even more confusing, Canada's definition of "Gluten" contains oats and other countries have their own definitions as well. This is actually a little misleading because studies have shown that it's not actually the oats themselves that have gluten but rather the process in which they are harvested and packaged that cause them to have gluten – a.k.a. cross contamination. So a good tip to remember is if the label only says "Wheat Free", chances are it's NOT gluten free (unless it's oats – but be sure to check with the manufacturer).

I've also recently been presented with the idea, from a few different individuals, that kamut is gluten free and people avoiding gluten can safely eat this grain. THIS IS NOT TRUE. Kamut is a derivative of wheat and although it has less gluten than wheat does and can be safely tolerated on a WHEAT FREE DIET, it should not be consumed if you are on a GLUTEN FREE DIET. Again, being informed is our greatest tool for our health.

## 3. Lacking a balanced diet

We've all heard the saying "everything in moderation". But I like to change that up a little – "all GOOD things in moderation". This also includes gluten free and vegan options. It's easy to think that because it's healthy, we can eat as much as we want and it's not going to affect us. As nice as this may seem, unfortunately that's not the case. Salad may be healthy but eating 5 plates of it certainly isn't! A good balance of fruits, vegetables, grains, nuts, seeds and plant-based proteins is definitely the way to go. And try to make your plate as colorful as possible with a variety of foods!

## 4. Gluten Free Junk Food

It's very easy to justify a maple-glazed donut or pecan tart that is gluten free. After all, it's just a treat, right? Of course it's nice to treat ourselves every now and again, but gluten free foods are just as capable of being junk food as their gluten-containing counterparts. It's not the gluten that makes them unhealthy – it's everything else: the sugar, fat, calories and sodium. And many gluten-free foods are guilty of putting in some, if not all, of those unhealthy ingredients.

It seems that more often than not, junk food is naturally gluten free! Many flavors of potato chips, candy, chocolate, popsicles, ice cream and soft drinks are all gluten-free by nature. That fact makes it very easy to reach for the not-so-good options. But there are a lot of healthy alternatives to traditional junk food. Try potato chips that are baked instead of deep fried or reach for a delicious trail mix instead of a bag of candy.

# 5. Gluten Free = Weight Loss.....or does it?

I will often hear of people that, when they decide to follow a gluten-free lifestyle, one of the side effects is weight loss. While this is definitely a common occurrence, it's not always the case. Many gluten-free options are high in refined carbohydrates, refined sugars, sodium and fat. These are not the ingredients for healthy weight-loss!

The key to keeping weight off is to not depend on pre-packaged foods and gluten free junk food (see

"Mistake #4") but to make things yourself. Although this is more time consuming, your efforts will not be in vain. By cooking things from scratch, you not only know what is in the food right down to the last ounce of salt, you also can tailor things to you and your family's preferences. And one other bonus to cooking your own meals: you save a TON of money. While you get thinner, your wallet gets fatter! That sounds like a win-win situation to me!

# Hidden Sources of Gluten

While labelling laws make it easier to identify if a particular product contains gluten or not, it's still a good idea to be well-informed as many countries have their own definition as to what constitutes "gluten free". Below, I've listed some products that may surprise you with the fact that they may contain gluten. This is not a complete list by any means – it's just a resource to get you started.

- Tortilla chips – "multi grain" varieties
- Vegan meat substitutes
- Cereals – often contain Barley Malt
- Some seasoning mixes
- Some salad dressings
- Certain flavors of ice cream (such as cherry cheesecake and cookies and cream)
- Seasoned French Fries and Hash Browns
- Oats (may contain wheat due to cross-contamination)
- Millet (while millet in itself is gluten free, be sure to use millet that is only certified gluten free – cross contamination issues similar to oats can be the problem)
- Some flavored teas and coffees
- Some makeup
- Foods cooked in the same oil or pans as gluten-containing foods at restaurants
- Soups – either in base or to thicken

- Vitamins, dietary supplements or medications
- Chinese food
- Household appliances – toasters and ovens
- Smoothies and yogurts with "cereals"
- Some soy and tamari sauce
- Malt vinegar
- Semolina
- Non-stick cooking sprays (can contain grain alcohol)
- Play-dough
- Some toothpastes
- Some shampoos/conditioners
- Some soaps

# Tips for Gluten Free Success

Below I've listed a few of my best tips for helping you have a successful experience living without gluten.  It can and will be challenging at times but if you stick with it and promise yourself you won't compromise no matter what, you'll be so happy in the end!

- Plan ahead – don't wait until the last minute to figure out what you're going to make/bring to a function.  It's almost always inevitable that there won't be a huge selection of gluten free options so make sure to plan to bring enough food so you won't be left with nothing.
- Try to always have frozen baked goods on hand (muffins, loaves, etc.).  They're easy to grab and go and there's very little preparation required.
- Find a Gluten free support group in your area.  If there isn't one in your town, there are many groups online that you can get support from.
- When at all possible, cook it yourself from scratch.  This eliminates any questioning or concern as to the safety of the ingredients.
- Cook gluten free for everyone in your house (as much as possible).  This might be hard and may not go over very well at first but trust me – it's SO much easier in the long run to not be trying to run a restaurant by giving everyone in your family a different meal!

- Use a variety of gluten free flours to replace wheat flour in a recipe. It's not a simple cup-for-cup replacement when it comes to gluten free baking. Experiment with a variety of gluten free flours to see which ones you like the best and which combinations work well together.

# Where are you getting your Fibre?

Whether you're avoiding gluten or not, getting adequate fibre is something that every person should be concerned about. Fibre has many health benefits and its intake has been linked to reducing the risk of heart disease, diabetes, obesity and certain types of cancer. A diet high in fibre also reduces the risk of gastrointestinal disorders and eases constipation and hemorrhoids as well as inflammatory bowel diseases including irritable bowel syndrome (IBS), Crohn's disease, ulcerative colitis and diverticulitis.

According to Health Canada, the RDI (Reference Daily Intake) of fibre is 38 g per day for men age 19-50, 30 g per day for men 51 and older, 25 g per day for women 19-50, and 21 g per day for women 51 and older. **In reality, though, the average Canadian is only taking in about 14 g per day.** Many other countries fall into the same category as more and more people are transitioning to a typical North American diet.

Fibre can be defined as a carbohydrate found in plants. But unlike other carbohydrates, it passes through the body undigested. That means fibre adds zero calories. Studies show that women who consumed more fibre were half as likely to be obese as those who consumed less fibre.

Unfortunately, most of what constitutes the typical North American diet is completely devoid of fibre – meats and sweets. Meat has absolutely no fibre and sweets are just empty calories lacking a whole lot of nutrition! When these make up the bulk of our daily food choices, it's pretty easy to see how one can be deficient in the all-important health factor – fibre.

When a doctor or dietitian makes a recommendation that you should add more fibre to your diet, the first things to be suggested are usually gluten-containing items such as bran or whole wheat products. This obviously poses a problem for anyone avoiding gluten. One of the largest complaints that I hear from those on a gluten-free diet is the lack of fibre once they've dispensed of such products as whole wheat bread, whole wheat pasta, bran flakes, all bran, etc.

So what kinds of food ARE high in fibre and also good for those avoiding gluten? Good sources of fibre can be mainly found in three areas: 1. grain products, including whole grains such as wild and brown rice and wheat free oats, 2. vegetables and fruit, and 3. Plant-based protein sources such as beans and lentils.

Below I've listed several good sources of fibre that can be easily added to our everyday diet.

- o ½ cup raspberries – 4 grams
- o 1 cup strawberry halves – 3 grams
- o 1 medium banana – 3.1 grams
- o 2 medium dried figs – 1.6 grams
- o 1 medium pear, including the peel – 5.5 grams

- 1 medium apple, including the peel – 4.4 grams
- 1 medium orange – 3.1 grams
- 1 oz (approx. 60) raisins – 1 gram
- 1 cup cooked split peas – 16.3 grams
- 1 cup cooked lentils – 15.6 grams
- 1 cup cooked black beans – 15 grams
- ¼ cup sunflower seed kernels – 3.9 grams
- 1 ounce of almonds – 3.5 grams
- 3 cups air-popped popcorn – 3.5 grams
- 56 grams (uncooked) brown rice pasta – 2 grams
- 1 Tbsp whole flax seed – 2.8 grams
- ¼ cup (uncooked) large flake oats – 2 grams
- ¼ cup (uncooked) steel cut oats – 4 grams
- 1 cup cooked green peas – 8.8 grams
- 1 small baked potato, with skin – 3 grams

Source: USDA National Nutrient Database for Standard Reference, 2012; Only Oats; Tinkyada

All fibre is not created equal, however. You may be familiar with the terms "soluble fibre" and "insoluble fibre". It is important that you understand the difference between these two types of fibre. While both of these fibres are important for preventing disease, proper digestion and overall health, they each have their own unique jobs. **_Soluble fibre_** binds with fatty acids and slows digestion so blood sugars are released more slowly into the body. Soluble fibre also helps lower cholesterol and helps regulate blood sugar levels for people with diabetes. **_Insoluble fibre_** helps to hydrate and move waste through the intestines. It also controls the pH levels in the intestines, a very important job for keeping us in good health. Insoluble fibre helps to prevent constipation and keeps your bowels regular.

The recommended consumption ratio is 25% soluble fibre and 75% insoluble fibre. The best sources of **soluble fibre** can be found in can be found in **vegetables and fresh fruit.** The best sources of **_insoluble fibre_** can be found in **_beans, flax seeds, chia seeds, whole oats and oat bran, psyllium seed husks, nuts, seeds, legumes, whole grains and cereals._**

If you're not already following a total vegetarian/vegan diet, Canada's Food Guide recommends that you have meat alternatives such as beans, lentils and tofu often. One Food Guide serving of a meat alternative is: 175 mL (3/4 cup) cooked legumes; 150g or 175mL (3/4 cup) tofu; 30 mL (2 tbsp) peanut or nut butters and 60 mL (1/4 cup) shelled nuts and seeds.

Here are some great tips for fibre success!:

- Choose a fibre-rich cereal. Granola or oatmeal made with wheat/gluten free oats is an excellent choice, especially steel cut oats or large flake oats.

- Eat more fruit and limit your intake of fruit juice. Don't forget that most of the fibre in fruit is in the peel!

- Increase your vegetables! Vegetables are low in calories and a good source of fibre and nutrition. And adding raw vegetables to your meals will really help to increase your fibre intake.

- Add legumes, seeds, sprouts and nuts into soups, salads, and stews.

- Eat less meat and more beans and plant-based foods. Remember: meat has no fibre so the more we fill up on meat, the less fibre we get.

- Add a couple of tablespoons of wheat/gluten free oat bran or ground flax to your baking.

- Use hummus as a spread on sandwiches instead of mustard or mayonnaise.

- Drink more water!  The more fibre you consume, the more water you need as well.  And when you wake up in the morning, drink 2 glasses of water right away to help get your body going.

- A great natural, gluten free bowel cleanser is this:

  o Take 1 Tbsp psyllium husks, mix it in 4-6 ounces of juice or smoothie and drink this immediately (don't leave very long as the psyllium will absorb the liquid and make it impossible to drink).  Do this 2-3 times/day.

  o Every other day, take 3 senna capsules or drink 1 cup of strong senna tea.

  o Please note that this is not something to be taken on a long-term basis but as a short term solution for occasional constipation or to achieve a mild bowel cleanse.  If taken on a long-term basis, it may result in a sluggish colon.

# Why Vegan/Vegetarian?

There can be any number of reasons for a person to choose to adopt a whole-food, plant-based diet.  Below, I've listed the main motivating factors.

- Environmental and Humanitarian Concerns
    - Raising animals uses a LOT of resources – space, water, food – just to name a few.  If a 10-acre farm grew soybeans it could feed 60 people, if it grew wheat it could feed 24 people and growing corn would feed 10 people. However, if it supported cattle it would only feed two people!

- Faith and Religious Reasons
    - Christianity – Mostly Seventh Day Adventists
    - Buddhism
    - Hinduism
    - Jainism
    - Sikhism
    - Islam – restricts pork consumption

- Animal Rights Beliefs
    - Many people who adopt a plant-based diet for this reason believe that the farming conditions that exist today are inhumane and are the cause of many illnesses, diseases and disfigurations among animals.  They strongly feel that those conditions are not ideal for animals nor do they feel that it is their place to use animals for food.

- Health Issues
  - Animal protein, fat and cholesterol all contribute to heart disease, certain cancers, diabetes, and other major chronic diseases. When someone is diagnosed with a disease, you will **<u>never</u>** hear them say "I ate more meat and my disease went away!". But what you will hear from those diagnosed with a disease, who choose to adopt a total plant-based diet, is story after story of improved health, improved mental clarity, weight loss and even totally being cured of their disease.

Plants Contain:
- ✓ Antioxidants
- ✓ Phytonutrients
- ✓ Vitamins
- ✓ Minerals
- ✓ Fibre
- ✓ Water

Meat has:
- ✗ Minimal nutrients
- ✗ No fibre
- ✗ Saturated fat
- ✗ Cholesterol
- ✗ Steroids
- ✗ Hormones
- ✗ High levels of pesticides
- ✗ Excess protein

# *Tips for starting a Plant-based diet:*

Studies have found that most families have about 9 consistent recipes that they rotate through. Below are some easy ideas for increasing your plant consumption!

1. Think of three vegan meals that you already enjoy – some ideas might be vegetable stir fry, pasta with marinara sauce, or tofu curry.

2. Think of three recipes that you already make that can easily be converted to vegan – veggie chili, lentil tacos, or black bean burgers are all delicious alternatives to traditional meals

3. Borrow or purchase vegan cookbooks and find 3 recipes that you and your family enjoy.

**In no time, you'll have 9 vegan meal options that you and your family will love!**

Here are some other tips that will help you on your way to eating more plant-based foods:

- Transition to a vegan diet with a daily fruit smoothie including some calcium-rich greens
- Switch from cow's milk to almond milk or other non-dairy substitute such as rice milk, soy milk or hemp milk
- Substitute organic tofu or beans in place of chicken
- Have one or two days per week where you cook "meatless"
- Dining out – try ethnic cuisines instead; more likely to find vegetarian and vegan options

# Menus & Recipes

# Picnic in the Park

Rosemary Corn Crackers
Curried Zucchini Hummus
Quinoa Tabbouleh
Quiche
Perfect Pie Crust
Thumbprint Cookies

"There are few things so pleasant as a picnic eaten in perfect comfort."

*William Somerset Maugham*

# Picnics

I don't know about you, but I know that in our house, as soon as the snow is gone and the ground is dry enough to sit on, we are digging out our picnic blanket and planning outdoor meals as much as possible.  There is something special about sharing a meal outdoors with family and friends.  The food somehow tastes extra good, the bugs don't seem quite so annoying and the sun shining just brings joy to our hearts.  I have included some easy picnicking menu ideas in this section to help get you outdoors and into nature.  They can all be prepared the day before and are all good served cold.  I hope you take some time to enjoy a few picnics and make a few memories!

# Rosemary Corn Crackers

Gluten free crackers can be both expensive and overloaded with sodium. If you're looking for a delicious snacking or dipping cracker, these are it! They are made with a lot less salt than commercial varieties but still have loads of flavor! Excellent with Hummus or just on their own.

Makes 24-30 crackers

## Ingredients:
- 1 ¼ cups water
- 1 ½ Tbsp tahini
- 1 ½ tsp salt
- 3 Tbsp nutritional yeast
- ½ cup unsalted cashews
- 1 Tbsp unsweetened coconut
- 1 tsp garlic powder
- 1 tsp onion powder
- 1 tsp dried, ground rosemary
- ½ cup water (additional amount)
- 1 ¼ cups corn meal

## Directions:
1. Preheat oven to 350*F. Blend first 9 ingredients together. When smooth, add additional ½ cup water and corn meal. Blend for a few seconds to mix.
2. Pour onto sprayed cookie sheet (one with edges)

3. Bake in preheated oven for 20 minutes.  Lightly slice into cracker-sized pieces and continue baking for an additional 40-45 minutes (don't cut all the way through).

# {Special Notes}

- Typically, rosemary is not ground.  If you're like me and prefer not having "sticks" of rosemary, simply grind dried rosemary in a coffee mill or blender until powdery.  This is the perfect consistency for this recipe.

# Curried Zucchini Hummus

Making the transition to a plant-based diet will, no doubt, cause some changes in our digestive system. Because meat and animal products are completely devoid of fibre, introducing fibre-rich foods such as legumes and beans can sometimes result in a bit of discomfort until our bodies get used to eating these healthful foods on a regular basis. This hummus recipe is a great transitional recipe because it gives you all the flavor of traditional hummus without the chick peas. It's the perfect picnic food because it goes great as a dip with *Rosemary Corn Crackers*, raw veggies, or as a spread on a sandwich.

Makes approximately 2 cups

## Ingredients:

- 1 ¼ cups peeled and chopped zucchini
- 1 Tbsp cold-pressed extra virgin olive oil
- Juice of 1 lemon (approximately 3-3 ½ Tbsp)
- 4-5 cloves garlic
- 1 tsp salt
- 1 tsp paprika
- ½ tsp cumin
- ½ cup tahini (sesame paste)
- 1/3 cup sesame seeds, soaked for 4-6 hours or overnight and drained

## Directions:

1. Combine all ingredients in a blender and blend until smooth and creamy. Store in an airtight container in the fridge.

# Quiche

Although this recipe is in my first book, I wanted to include it here because it's such a great addition to picnics as it can be served either hot or cold.

Makes 1-9" Quiche

## Ingredients:

- 1 -420g package firm tofu, NOT silken or extra firm
- 1 pkg frozen spinach, thawed and excess water squeezed out
- 1/2 zucchini, diced
- ½ cup sliced green onions
- 1 medium green pepper, diced
- 1 cup fresh, sliced mushrooms
- 1/3 cup nutritional yeast flakes
- 2-3 Tbsp Chicken Style Seasoning *(See Miscellaneous)*
- 2-3 Tbsp cold pressed, extra virgin olive oil
- 1-2 cups vegan cheddar-style shredded cheese such as Daiya, optional
- 1 recipe Perfect Pie Crust, rolled and pressed into a 9" pie plate, unbaked (see this section)

## Directions:

1. Preheat oven to 350*F.  Drain and rinse tofu and mash or crumble with your hands into a large bowl.
2. In a large frying pan, sauté zucchini, peppers, green onions and mushrooms in a little water until softened.  Add vegetables and all remaining ingredients to tofu.  Mix well and pack into unbaked pie shell(s).
3. Bake in preheated oven for 50-60 minutes or until firm with moisture gone.  If the quiche is still slightly moist, put under the broiler for a few minutes but watch carefully so the crust doesn't burn!

# Quinoa Tabbouleh

Traditionally, Tabbouleh is made with bulgur wheat and lots of parsley. This gluten free version can be easily served as an entrée or a side dish and makes a wonderful option for a picnic or potluck.

Makes 10-12 servings

## Ingredients:

- 1 cup uncooked quinoa
- 1 Tbsp Chicken-style seasoning *(See Seasonings and Extras)*
- 2 cups water
- 2 medium tomatoes, seeded and chopped
- ½ English cucumber, quartered and chopped
- 3 cloves garlic, minced
- 3 green onions, chopped
- 1 cup chopped fresh parsley
- 1-1 ½ tsp salt
- Juice of 1 lemon (approximately ¼-1/3 cup)
- Zest of 1 lemon
- ¼-1/3 cup extra virgin olive oil (cold pressed is best)

## Directions:

1. Place quinoa, Chicken-style seasoning and water in a medium pot. Bring to a boil over high heat, cover, reduce heat and simmer for 20 minutes. Remove from heat, transfer to a serving bowl and allow to cool until room temperature or colder.
2. Once quinoa has cooled, add remaining ingredients and stir well.

3. Refrigerate for at least 4 hours before serving. Stir briefly again before serving.

# {Special Notes}

- It's best to cook the quinoa the night before or make this salad in the morning to allow time for the ingredients to cool and to chill.
- Tastes even better the next day! Serve with baked potatoes topped with Sunflower Sour Cream and chives and steamed mixed vegetables for a meal that takes very little preparation and tastes wonderful.
- This is an excellent "garden-to-table" recipe. Fresh garden vegetables give any recipe increased flavor and nutrients!

# Perfect Pie Crust

I call this "Perfect Pie Crust" because it doesn't have to chill, it rolls out beautifully and tastes great! Perfect!

Makes enough for 1 double crust pie

## Ingredients:

- 1 cup sorghum flour
- ½ cup tapioca starch
- ¼ cup chick pea flour
- 2 Tbsp potato starch (NOT flour)
- 2 Tbsp arrowroot starch
- ½ cup + 2 Tbsp all vegetable shortening, cool or cold is best
- 1 tsp xanthan gum
- 1 tsp salt
- 4-8 Tbsp cold water

## Directions:

1. In a medium bowl, mix together the flours, starches, xanthan gum and salt. Cut in shortening and mix with a pastry blender until crumbs form.
2. Add cold water, 2 Tbsp at a time until desired consistency is reached. You want it to be holding together when you squeeze it but not at all sticky.
3. Form into two balls. Place one sheet of waxed paper on countertop that's been lightly moistened with water. This helps the waxed paper stick to the counter and not move around.
4. Place ball of dough on waxed paper and place another sheet of waxed paper on top. Roll dough to desired size and thickness.

5. Remove the top sheet of waxed paper and place the pie plate face down on the pastry. With your hand underneath the bottom sheet of waxed paper, gently lift the pastry into the pie plate while at the same time turning the pie plate over. Press down the pastry into the plate and gently remove the other sheet of waxed paper.
6. Flute edges or press down with a fork and trim the sides of the pie crust with a sharp knife.
7. For prebaked crusts, prick the bottom and sides with a fork a few times and bake in preheated 350*F oven for 10 minutes or until golden.

# Thumbprint Cookies

If you're looking for a delicious cookie that is free of refined sugars, look no further!  It's a good thing this recipe makes a lot because you can't just stop at 1!

Makes 50-60 cookies

## Ingredients:

- 4 1/4 cups wheat free oats, ground finely (or use 4 cups wheat free oat flour)
- 2 cups pecan meal (grind pecans in a food processor or purchase pre-ground pecans)
- 1 cup honey
- ½ cup vegetable oil
- ¼ cup water
- 1 Tbsp cornstarch
- ½ tsp sea salt
- 2 Tbsp pure vanilla extract
- Strawberry jam (or flavor of your choice), naturally sweetened if possible

## Directions:

1. Preheat oven to 350*F.
2. In a large bowl, combine ground oats and ground nuts.  Add remaining ingredients (except jam) and stir well.
3. Let the dough sit for 10 minutes.  It should be just firm enough to shape into balls with wet hands.  If the dough is too sticky, add a little more oat flour (dough should be slightly sticky however).

4. Roll into balls and place on sprayed cookie sheet. Slightly damp hands work best here. Alternatively, you can use a cookie scoop (1/2-1 Tbsp size). Press thumb into the center of each cookie before baking. Add a small amount of jam to each indent.
5. Bake for 8-10 minutes or until lightly browned. Let sit for 5-10 minutes then remove carefully from the cookie sheet to cool. Cookies will harden as they cool.

# *Christmas Dinner*

Garlic Baked Squash
Braised Peas
Baked Rice Loaf
Mashed Potatoes Supreme
Mushroom Gravy
Cheesecake with Raspberry Sauce

"Wise men still seek Him."
*Unknown*

# Christmas

Nativity scenes….snow….carols…..jingle bells….Christmas cookies baking…many things conjure up memories of Christmas.  The true meaning of Christmas, however - remembering that Jesus came to earth to save us from our sins - is slowly being pushed away in favor of a more commercial and materialistic holiday.  It's easy to get trapped into the busyness and chaos of the Christmas season but let's remember that it's not about how many gifts we give or receive, how many Christmas cards we send or get in the mail or even about how delicious the food is or keeping the family traditions alive.  It's about simplicity, peace, stillness and love.  Why not invite a lonely widow that you know over for Christmas dinner?  Or how about the neighbor down the street with a young family that just lost his job?  Although they may not remember what you serve that night, they will remember your kindness and love.  That is the true meaning of Christmas after all, isn't it?

# Baked Garlic Squash

Squash is slowly becoming a favorite in my books. I never used to like it but I'm sure that's because I never had it prepared in a delicious way such as this simple, flavorful dish!

Makes 6 servings

## Ingredients:

- 2 Tbsp cold-pressed extra virgin olive oil
- 3-4 garlic cloves, minced
- 1 tsp salt
- 3 ½ pounds butternut squash, peeled and cut into cubes.

## Directions:

1. Preheat oven to 400*F. Place prepared squash into a 2-quart baking dish.
2. Combine oil, minced garlic and salt in a small bowl and add to squash. Stir well to coat.
3. Bake in preheated oven for 50-55 minutes, stirring 2-3 times.

## {Special Notes}

- The word "squash" comes from a Native American term "askutasquash" which translates to "eaten raw or uncooked".
- Summer Squash – like zucchini or crookneck - and Winter Squash – such as butternut, hubbard, or pumpkin - varieties are both readily available and can be cooked in so many ways – baked, fried, boiled, or steamed – just to name a few!
- Squash is very high in vitamin A and a great source of iron, calcium and potassium.

# Braised Peas

Peas, onions and......what?  Cooked lettuce??  Don't let that ingredient scare you away!  It's actually really tasty and reminiscent of steamed spinach.  Give this recipe a try and serve your guests something different for the holidays!

Makes 4-6 servings

## Ingredients:

- 1-1 ½ Tbsp cold pressed extra virgin olive oil
- 2 Tbsp brown rice flour
- 1 ¼ cups water mixed with ½ Tbsp Chicken-Style seasoning (*See Seasonings and Extras*)
- 1 bunch green onions chopped (about 6)
- 3 cups fresh or frozen peas
- ½ medium head red leaf lettuce or other tender lettuce, chopped into ribbons
- sea salt
- freshly squeezed lemon juice

## Directions:

1. Pour the olive oil into a frying pan.  Over medium-low heat make a roux by adding the flour to the olive oil.  Stir with a whisk, then slowly pour in the water mixed with the Chicken-style seasoning.
2. Increase the heat to medium and add the onions, peas and lettuce.  Cover and simmer for 5 minutes or until vegetables are tender and sauce is thickened.
3. Add salt to taste and serve drizzled with a splash of freshly squeezed lemon juice.

# Baked Rice Loaf

Warm, comforting and delicious best describes this loaf. Top with gravy and serve alongside your favorite vegetable for a delicious holiday meal that's sure to be a new family favorite.

Makes 1 loaf/casserole

## Ingredients:

- 4 cups cooked brown rice (about 1 ½ cups uncooked rice)
- 1 cup ground pecans
- 2 cups ground wheat-free quick oats
- 1 large onion, chopped finely
- 2 tsp salt
- 2 Tbsp Nutritional yeast flakes
- 1 tsp garlic powder
- 1 tsp oregano
- 1 tsp celery seed
- 1 Tbsp basil
- ½ cup hot water

## Directions:

1. Cook rice according to package directions. Set aside in a large mixing bowl.
2. Preheat oven to 350*F. In food processor, grind pecans. Place in bowl with rice. Do the same with the wheat-free oats.
3. Cut onion into large chunks and place in food processor. Pulse several times until finely chopped but not minced. Place in bowl with rice and add remaining ingredients. Mix well.
4. Oil a 3-quart casserole dish or large bread pan. Pour rice mixture into baking dish and smooth the top level.
5. Bake in preheated oven for 45-55 minutes.
6. Serve hot with *Mushroom Gravy* (see recipe in this section).

# Mashed Potatoes Supreme

This is a great side dish that combines 4 vegetables into one – carrots, turnips, onion and potatoes. It's important to cut the carrots and turnips into small dices so they cook in the same amount of time as the potatoes. Alternatively, you can cook it all in a pressure cooker and they come out beautifully done in only 5-7 minutes.

Makes 6-8 servings

## Ingredients:

- 1 turnip, peeled and diced into 1/2" cubes
- 4 carrots, peeled and diced
- 1 large onion, chopped
- 6 medium-large potatoes, peeled and cubed
- Non-hydrogenated vegan margarine, to taste
- Unflavored Non-dairy milk of your choice
- Salt to taste

## Directions:

1. Prepare vegetables and place all together in a large pot (or pressure cooker). Cover with water and bring to a boil. Cover and simmer until tender, about 20-30 minutes.
2. If you're using a pressure cooker, consult your cooker's instruction manual to know how much water and time is required. Use the time suggested for the vegetable that has the longest cooking time.
3. When fully cooked, remove from heat, drain and mash with a potato masher. Add margarine and salt. Mix with an electric mixer and add enough non-dairy milk to reach desired consistency.

# Mushroom Gravy

Gravy in a plant-based cookbook?  Sure!  The cashew base in this delicious gravy gives it a robust and nutty flavor that complements many dishes perfectly.  Serve it over Baked Rice Loaf, mashed potatoes or oven-baked fries for a wonderfully warming meal.

Makes 5 1/2 cups

## Ingredients:

- 1 cup unsalted cashews
- 4 cups water
- ½ cup brown rice flour
- 1 Tbsp onion powder
- 1 tsp garlic powder
- 1 Tbsp gluten free soy sauce
- 1 tsp lemon juice
- 1 tsp dried basil
- 1/8 tsp dried ground rosemary
- 1 tsp salt
- 2 tsp dried parsley
- 1 can mushroom pieces, drained

## Directions:

1. Place all ingredients except mushrooms in blender and blend until smooth.  Add mushrooms and pulse 1-2 times just to slightly chop.
2. Pour into large saucepan and thicken over medium heat, stirring constantly with a wire whisk.  Serve hot.

1. Blend all ingredients with 2 cups of the water in blender.

2. Pour into large saucepan.  Pour remaining 2 cups water in blender and blend for a few seconds.  This "cleans" the blender out and helps you not to waste any of the gravy.  Pour water into pot with the rest of the gravy mixture.
3. Cook over medium heat, stirring constantly until thick.  Remove from heat and serve.

# Cheesecake with Raspberry Sauce

"Cheesecake" you ask?  How is that possible without cream cheese? If you thought that having a plant-based diet meant an end to creamy, luscious cheesecake then I'm happy to say that it doesn't have to be that way!  Be forewarned, though, that it is very rich so it's best to save it for special occasions.

Makes 1-8" cheesecake

## Ingredients:

### Crust:

- 2 cups macadamia nuts (raw is best) or walnuts, soaked for 4-6 hours, drained and rinsed
- ½ cup dates
- ¼ cup unsweetened coconut

### Filling:

- 1 ¼ cups cashews (raw is best), soaked for 4-6 hours, drained and rinsed
- ¼ cup + 2 Tbsp warmed, scented coconut oil
- ¼ cup lime or lemon juice
- ¼ cup maple syrup
- 1 Tbsp pure vanilla extract

### Raspberry Sauce:

- 2 cups raspberries, fresh or frozen and thawed
- 1 Tbsp lemon juice
- 3 Tbsp cane sugar
- Additional fresh raspberries for garnish

# To make the Crust:

1. Place soaked and drained macadamia nuts or walnuts in a food processor that has been fitted with the "S" blade. Add dates and coconut and pulse until mixture resembles crumbs and the dates are sticking the whole mixture together. Add a small amount of water, if needed, to stick mixture together.
2. In an 8" springform pan that has been lined with parchment paper, pour crust mixture and press down evenly along the bottom and up the sides slightly. Place in the refrigerator while you make the filling.

# To make the Filling:

1. Place soaked and rinsed cashews, liquefied coconut oil, lime or lemon juice, maple syrup, vanilla and ¼ cup + 2 Tbsp water into blender. Process until smooth and creamy.
2. Pour mixture into chilled crust and freeze for 2-3 hours or until firm.
3. Remove from the freezer and place in the refrigerator for an hour before serving. Top with Raspberry Sauce.

# To make the Raspberry Sauce:

1. Place raspberries and lemon juice in a blender and puree until smooth. If you prefer a smoother sauce, strain through a fine sieve or cheesecloth.
2. Stir in sugar. Pour over individual cheesecake slices and top with additional raspberries.

# Notes:

# *Happy Birthday!*

Creamy Pasta Bake
Mini Pizzas
Pizza Sauce
Yogurt Yum-Yum Popsicles
Orange Delight Cupcakes
Cherry Fudgesicles or Ice Cream

"Life is a succession of lessons which must be lived to be understood."

*Helen Keller*

# Happy Birthday!

It's always challenging for children who have food allergies to be able to enjoy fun birthday party food. I remember when I was growing up, the typical party food consisted of hotdogs, boxed Macaroni and Cheese, cake and ice cream. While this might be kid-pleasing foods, it's not so nice if you have an allergy or have chosen a lifestyle that avoids these things.

I know how it is to live with multiple food allergies and when you add in a plant-based diet, it's rare to be able to eat what has been prepared at parties. I can also understand how appreciated it is when someone takes the time to plan a meal that is suitable for all in attendance. In this section, I've included some kid-friendly choices like mini-pizzas, cupcakes, ice cream and pasta. But don't think that you have to be a kid to enjoy them! All of these options are naturally wheat, gluten, egg, dairy, lactose and meat free so your guests can be rest assured that you have their best interests in mind and can sit back and have fun without worrying about what they're going to eat!

# Creamy Pasta Bake

Pasta, in any form, is a favorite in our house.  Gluten free varieties are becoming more available and are tasting better than ever.  For best results in this recipe, slightly undercook your pasta to avoid having a mushy final product.

Makes 8-10 servings

## Ingredients:

- 1 lb uncooked pasta (corkscrew or penne work great)
- 1 cup frozen peas
- 1 small zucchini
- ½ lb fresh mushrooms or 1 can mushrooms
- 1 red or green pepper
- ¾ cup cashews
- 2 Tbsp Chicken Style Seasoning (See *Seasonings and Extras*)
- 1 tsp garlic powder
- 2 tsp onion powder
- 5 cups water, divided
- ¼ cup + 1 Tbsp brown rice flour
- ½ tsp salt
- ¼ cup tahini

## Directions:

1. Cook noodles until almost done.  A good method that works with rice pasta is to boil the water, add the noodles, stir and turn off the stove.  Let sit, covered, in hot water for 10 minutes.  Drain and rinse with cold water.  Pour into a large casserole dish that has been sprayed with cooking spray.  Set aside.

2. Meanwhile, sauté zucchini, mushrooms, and red or green pepper in a small amount of water until soft. Pour on top of noodles in casserole dish. Add peas and set aside.

3. In a blender, combine cashews, seasonings, 3 cups water, flour, salt and tahini. Blend until smooth and creamy.

4. Pour into a large saucepan. Pour the remaining 2 cups of water into blender. Pulse a few times and pour water into saucepan with the rest of the gravy. This step helps to "clean out" the blender and not waste any of the gravy.

5. Over medium-high heat, thicken the gravy, stirring constantly. Once thickened, pour over noodle mixture and stir well.

6. Bake at 350*F for 20-30 minutes or until heated through and bubbly.

# {Special Notes}

- To add some "crunch" to this casserole, coarsely crush gluten free corn flakes (enough to make 2 cups) and sprinkle over the top of the noodles before baking. Corn flakes should be lightly browned when done.

# Mini Pizzas

Kids love having their own individual pizzas!  Having kids choose their own toppings and eagerly await to sample their creations makes a great birthday activity and also helps cut down some of your preparation time.

Makes 8 Mini Pizzas

## Ingredients:

- 1 recipe Pizza Sauce (see this section)
- Toppings of your choice
    - Green peppers
    - Fresh mushrooms
    - Broccoli, chopped fine
    - Green olives
    - Pineapple tidbits
    - Sautéed onions
    - Thinly sliced tomatoes
- 1 pkg Daiya mozzarella-style cheese shreds
- 4 Gluten, Dairy, and Egg Free English Muffins, thawed and cut in half lengthwise (Food For Life brand offers a Gluten Free/Vegan product); alternatively, you can use slices of thawed gluten free/vegan bread.

## Directions:

1. Prepare Pizza Sauce according to recipe instructions.  Set aside until ready to use.
2. Chop vegetables finely and place in individual bowls.  Set aside.
3. Thaw and split English Muffins so you have 8 individual "pizza crusts"

4. Preheat oven to 350*F.
5. Spread desired amount of pizza sauce on each crust.  At this point, you can either place the toppings on yourself or allow the children to help you with this.
6. Top with Daiya cheese and place individual pizzas on a cookie sheet.
7. Bake in preheated oven for 15-20 minutes or until heated through.

# {Special Notes}

- These pizzas freeze wonderfully!  Make up some extras but don't bake them.  Place them between waxed paper in an airtight container and freeze for up to 3 months.  You can bake the frozen pizzas at 350*F for 30 minutes.

# Pizza Sauce

My mom taught me many things in the kitchen while I was growing up. She shared with me much advice, tips and recipes – including this one.

Makes 2 cups

## Ingredients:

- 1 onion, chopped in small pieces
- 1 5.5 oz can tomato paste
- ½ quart canned tomatoes, undrained
- 1 tsp dried basil
- 1 tsp dried oregano
- 1 tsp garlic powder
- 1 tsp onion salt OR a combination of 1 tsp onion powder and ½-3/4 tsp salt

## Directions:

1. Place onion in a frying pan or medium saucepan with a small amount of water. Sautee onion in water until soft. Add tomato paste, tomatoes, basil, oregano, garlic powder and onion salt.
2. Simmer for about ½ hour. This is enough for one pizza but it does make a fair amount. Any leftover sauce freezes well.

# Yogurt Yum-Yum Popsicles

These popsicles were always a favorite of mine growing up. Originally they were made with cow's milk yogurt but coconut milk yogurt is a delicious alternative that can be used in its place.

Makes 375 mL

## Ingredients:
- 1 454g tub Plain Cultured Coconut Milk Yogurt (So Delicious is our favorite)
- ½ cup orange juice concentrate (NOT diluted)
- Honey or vanilla, to taste, optional

## Directions:
1. Combine yogurt, orange juice concentrate and optional honey and vanilla in a large bowl. Stir well until mixed.
2. Spoon into popsicle moulds and freeze for several hours or overnight.
3. Run popsicle mould under hot water for a few seconds to release them.

# Orange Delight Cupcakes

For anyone who has a child suffering from a gluten, dairy, egg, or nut allergy, these make a wonderful treat for a birthday or other special occasion.

Makes 18 cupcakes

## Ingredients:
- 1 cup + 2 Tbsp sorghum flour
- ¾ cup sifted coconut flour
- 1 cup + 2 Tbsp tapioca starch
- 1 cup cane sugar or coconut sugar (white sugar is fine too, it's just a lot more processed)
- ½ tsp salt
- 1 ½ tsp gluten free baking powder
- 1 ½ tsp gluten free baking soda
- 1 ½ tsp xanthan gum
- ¾ cup coconut milk
- ½ Tbsp lemon juice
- 1 ½ cups warm water
- ¼ cup vegetable oil
- ½ tsp orange extract
- Zest of 1 orange
- 1 ½ Tbsp pure vanilla extract
- Scant ½ cup unsweetened applesauce

## Icing:
- ½ cup all-vegetable shortening
- ½ cup vegan margarine (Earth Balance or Vegan Becel)
- 4 cups icing sugar (many brands are naturally gluten free)

- ½-3/4 tsp pure vanilla extract
- ¼ tsp almond extract
- Zest of 1 orange
- Juice of 1 orange or as much as needed

## Directions:

1. Preheat oven to 375*F. Pour coconut milk into 4 cup measuring cup. Add lemon juice and set aside.
2. Meanwhile, grease muffin tins. Alternatively, you can line with cupcake papers but be forewarned that any kind of baking that is done without eggs tends to stick to muffin papers. If you prefer decorative cupcake papers, try spraying the liners after you've put them in the tins.
3. In a large bowl, mix together dry ingredients.
4. Add warm water, vegetable oil, vanilla, orange extract, orange zest (first amount) and applesauce to coconut milk mixture. Mix well and add to dry ingredients.
5. Mix with electric mixer on medium-high until smooth. A large countertop mixer works best for this but a handheld mixer will do fine as well. The batter is thick so you will just have to watch it carefully when mixing.
6. Scoop into sprayed muffin tins and bake in preheated oven for 15-20 minutes or until light brown on top and cake tester comes out clean.
7. To make the icing, place margarine and vegetable shortening in a bowl. Add extracts and icing sugar. Mix with electric mixer, starting on low and then increasing the speed as the mixture gets thicker. Add enough orange juice to get it to the desired consistency (usually only a couple of Tablespoons at most).
8. You can either scoop the icing into a piping bag that has been fitted with a "1-M" tip and pipe swirls on the top of each cupcake or you can simply spread the icing on with a spatula. Add gluten free sprinkles or colored sugar of your choice.

# Cherry Fudgesicles or Ice Cream

Fudgesicles or Ice Cream?  What a tough decision!  This dual-duty recipe can serve as either – or both!

Makes 6 servings of ice cream

## Ingredients:

- 1 398-mL can full-fat coconut milk, chilled
- 1 tsp peanut butter, almond butter or soy nut butter (omit if you just want cherry ice cream)
- 3 sliced, frozen bananas
- 2 ½ Tbsp carob powder (omit if you just want cherry ice cream)
- 12 dates, soaked for 1-2 hours if you don't have a powerful blender
- 2 cups frozen pitted cherries
- 1 Tbsp almond extract

## Directions:

1. Combine all ingredients except cherries in a blender.
2. Add cherries and pulse a few times until cherries have reached the desired size.
3. At this point, you have 3 options: 1. Spoon into popsicle moulds and freeze for several hours or until firm; 2. Pour into frozen ice cream maker drum and process according to your machine's directions; 3. Pour into glasses immediately and eat with a spoon!

## {Special Notes}

- A fun way to serve this for a child's birthday party is to give each child their own individual Dixie cup full of ice cream. Have a variety of gluten free colored sugar or sprinkles available for them to top their ice cream with.
- There is an increasing number of gluten free/allergy friendly ice cream cones available. If you want a special treat, pick up a package of cones and your children will be thrilled to have an ice cream cone again!
- An ice cream maker is definitely beneficial in making coconut milk ice creams. You can also blend the ingredients and use it straight out of the blender but the consistency will be much softer.
- Coconut milk ice cream is best eaten fresh. If you try to freeze it, it turns into one solid brick which makes it very difficult to scoop out!

# Thanksgiving

Stamppot Carrots
Roasted Root Vegetables
Sauteed Greens
Green Bean Casserole
Stuffing
Savory Baked Tofu
Maple Pecan Tarts

"For health and food, for love and friends, for everything Thy goodness sends; Father in Heaven, we thank Thee."

*Ralph Waldo Emmerson*

# *Thanksgiving*

Thanksgiving is one of those holidays that, to me, has many wonderful memories tied to it.  In Canada, Thanksgiving is in October and that's usually right when all the gardening is finishing up, when the days are getting shorter and cooler, frost is in the air and leaves are changing to their beautiful fall hues.  It's also the time when we sit back and enjoy a wonderful Thanksgiving meal, thanking the Lord for the bounty of the year.  "But", some may say, "you can't have Thanksgiving without turkey!"  Having a delicious Thanksgiving meal without the traditional turkey and stuffing is still possible!  Maple Pecan Tarts topped with crunchy maple-glazed pecans, Green Bean Casserole in a savory mushroom sauce, wonderful fall root vegetables roasted with garlic and herbs – these are just some of my ideas for making your plant-based, gluten free Thanksgiving Dinner one to remember!

# Stamppot Carrots

In my first cookbook, I explain that Stamppot is translated as "mash pot" and is a traditional Dutch dish that is usually a combination of potatoes, vegetables or greens such as kale or Swiss chard. Another option, which I have here, is to use carrots instead of greens and add some savory herbs. This gives this made-vegan dish all the flavor of traditional stamppot without the fat, cholesterol or meat.

Makes 6-8 servings

## Ingredients:

- 3 large carrots, peeled and sliced
- 3 pounds potatoes, peeled, washed and cut into large chunks
- 2 bay leaves
- ½ tsp dried sage
- ¼ tsp dried savory
- 1 tsp chicken-style seasoning (See *Seasonings and Extras*)
- 2 tsp salt
- 3 Tbsp non-hydrogenated vegan margarine
- Cooking water to mash

## Directions:

1. Place carrots, potatoes and bay leaves in a large pot. Cover with water and cook until carrots and potatoes are tender.
2. Drain water into a separate container, reserving for mashing. Discard bay leaves.
3. Mash potatoes with remaining ingredients. Add enough of the cooking water to give you the desired consistency.

# {*Special Notes*}

It's important that the carrots be significantly smaller than the potatoes as it takes far longer for carrots to cook than it does potatoes. To avoid having underdone carrots, slice them in ¼ inch rounds and cut the potatoes in large chunks. Alternatively, you could use a pressure cooker. This will cook everything adequately and in a shorter amount of time.

# Roasted Root Vegetables

So many wonderful root vegetables are included in this recipe. This dish is perfect for Thanksgiving so although it is in my first cookbook, I knew I had to include it in here as well.

Makes 6-8 servings

## Ingredients:

- 1 pound sweet potatoes
- 1 pound parsnips
- 1 pound turnips
- 1 pound carrots
- 2 Tbsp chopped fresh rosemary or 1 tsp dried, ground rosemary
- 3 tbsp chopped fresh sage or 2 tsp dried, rubbed sage (less if using ground sage)
- ¼-1/3 cup cold pressed extra virgin olive oil
- 1 head garlic, minced
- 1-2 tsp coarse sea or kosher salt or to taste

## Directions:

1. Preheat oven to 400*F.  Peel and cut all vegetables into 1-inch pieces.  Combine all ingredients in large roasting pan and toss to combine.  Season with salt.
2. Roast for 1-1 ¼ hours, uncovered, stirring occasionally.

## {Special Notes}

- Chunks of potatoes, onions, cauliflower, brussel sprouts, fennel bulbs or cabbage are also great additions to this mix.

# Sauteed Greens

"Greens" (a.k.a. Swiss Chard, Spinach, Kale, Mustard Greens, etc.) are so underrated!  We need to include more of these nutritional powerhouses in our daily diet!  They are high in calcium, fibre and a host of vitamins and minerals.

Makes 6-8 servings

## Ingredients:

- 8 cups chopped greens – Swiss Chard, Kale, Spinach, Mustard Greens, etc.
- 6 cloves garlic, minced
- ½ tsp salt or to taste
- ½-3/4 tsp garlic powder
- ¼ cup gluten free meatless bacon bits, optional but really adds a nice smoked flavor

## Directions:

1. In a large frying pan, sauté the garlic in a little water until soft. Add greens and sauté for 5-7 minutes or until wilted and soft. Depending on the type of green you choose will determine how reduced they get.
2. Saute until all the water has evaporated, watching carefully so as to not burn your greens.
3. Place cooked greens in a serving bowl and add salt, garlic powder and optional meatless bacon bits.  Stir to combine.

# Green Bean Casserole

If you've never had this warm and comforting dish before, imagine green beans baked in a creamy mushroom sauce....absolutely delicious!

Makes 6-8 servings

## Ingredients:

- 4-398 mL cans green beans, drained
- ¾ cup cashews
- 1/3 cup brown rice flour
- 2 Tbsp onion powder
- 1 ½ tsp salt, or to taste
- 1 lb fresh mushrooms, finely diced
- 1 medium onion, finely diced
- 4 cups water
- 1 small onion, sliced into rings
- ½ cup cornmeal
- 2 Tbsp brown rice flour, additional amount
- ½ tsp salt
- 2 Tbsp light olive oil

## Directions:

1. Place drained beans in a large casserole dish.  Set aside
2. In a blender, combine cashews, first amount of rice flour, onion powder, salt and 2 cups water. Blend on high speed until smooth and creamy.  If your blender is not very powerful, you may want to soak your cashews overnight first.
3. In a saucepan over medium heat, sauté onions and mushrooms in a little water until tender. Reduce heat to medium-low, pour

blended cashew into the saucepan with the onions, add the remaining water ½ cup at a time and stir with a whisk until it reaches desired thickness. You may not use all the water.

4. Pour thickened mushroom sauce over beans and set aside while you make the onion rings for the top.

5. In a large resealable plastic bag, combine freshly sliced onion rings, cornmeal, 2 Tbsp brown rice flour and salt. Shake well to coat evenly.

6. Heat the olive oil in a frying pan over medium heat. Add the coated onions and brown for 6-8 minutes or until brown and crispy, turning with a spatula or metal tongs every couple of minutes.

7. Place onion rings on top of casserole. You may not use them all depending on the size and shape of your casserole dish. Bake in a preheated 350*F oven for 30 minutes or until heated through and lightly browned on top.

# Stuffing

When my sister-in-law and I visited Burlington, Ontario, we were privileged to visit a great gluten free and vegan bakery called "Kelly's Bake Shoppe". They are also an organic, peanut-free, egg-free, dairy-free and soy-free bakery that serves delicious cupcakes, cookies and other treats! Kelly Childs and Erinn Weatherbie (a mother and daughter team!) also have a wonderful gluten free and vegan restaurant in Burlington called Kindfood. This recipe is one of Kelly's and I know you will enjoy having a delicious and savory stuffing to add to your Gluten Free and Vegan Thanksgiving table!

## Ingredients:

- 11 cups of fresh or stale Gluten Free and Vegan ½" bread cubes
- 2 tbsp + 1 tbsp olive oil (go for a good quality brand)
- 1 tbsp non-hydrogenated vegan margarine, such as Earth Balance
- 1 tbsp fresh garlic, minced
- 1 cup finely chopped onion
- 1 ½ cup finely chopped celery
- ½ cup finely chopped parsley
- 1/8 cup finely chopped fresh thyme
- 1 tsp dry rubbed sage
- 1 tsp dried thyme
- Sea salt to taste
- 2-3 cups vegetable stock

## Directions:

1. Preheat oven to 400*F. Toast bread cubes on a large baking sheet until golden brown. Set aside for 5-10 minutes.

2. Heat 2 tbsp of olive oil and 1 tbsp of Earth Balance in a large skillet over medium heat.   Saute onions, garlic, and celery until soft.
3. Put sautéed vegetables into bowl with toasted bread cubes and mix, preferably by hand.
4. Add thyme, parsley, sage and dried thyme and salt.
5. Drizzle with olive oil and stir well.
6. Add 2 cups of vegetable stock and mix until absorbed. Add another cup gradually until the mixture becomes moist but NOT soggy.
7. Bake in a covered casserole dish for 25 minutes. You can also uncover the casserole dish at the end to brown the stuffing for 5-10 minutes.

# {*Special Notes*}

- A special thanks to Kelly Childs for allowing me to include this recipe in my cookbook.  For more information on Kelly's Bake Shoppe and Kindfood, visit www.kellysbakeshoppe.com or www.kindfood.com.

# Savory Baked Tofu

Tofu seems to have a bad reputation among meat-eaters and new-to-the-plant-scene individuals. It's a popular view that tofu is tasteless and the texture is strange, leaving little to be desired by those who want to try something new. Baking tofu gives it a great texture and the simple seasonings of this dish create a delicious flavour that makes meat-eaters and vegan/vegetarians alike come back for more!

Makes 10-12 pieces

## Ingredients:

- 1 pkg Extra firm tofu, drained and rinsed
- Chicken-style seasoning (See *Seasonings and Extras*)
- Olive oil

## Directions:

1. Slice tofu into ½" pieces. Lay them flat in a 9x13 baking dish.
2. Sprinkle chicken-style seasoning on top of each piece. Brush with olive oil.
3. Flip tofu pieces over and repeat.
4. Let marinate for 2-3 hours in the refrigerator.
5. Preheat oven to 350*F.
6. Bake tofu for 20 minutes. Flip pieces over and return to the oven for another 20-25 minutes or until cooked to desired firmness.

# Maple Pecan Tarts

Do you think it's possible to have delicious pecan tarts without them being full of refined sugars and empty calories?  I'm here to tell you it is!  There is also another secret ingredient that will surprise your guests – flax seeds!  No one will ever know if you don't tell them!

Makes 24 tarts

## Ingredients:

- 1 ½ cups pecans, whole or slightly broken
- 2-3 Tbsp pure maple syrup
- 1 ½ cups water
- 6 Tbsp ground flaxseed
- 1 cup pure maple syrup
- 1 ½ cups dates
- 1 tsp pure vanilla extract
- 1 tsp maple extract
- 1 tsp salt
- 1/3 cup water
- 6 Tbsp cornstarch
- 1 recipe *Perfect Pie Crust* (see *Picnic in the Park* section) OR 1 pkg The Mix Company *Pastry Perfection* Pie Crust Mix

To prepare the mix, you will need:
- Shortening
- Salt
- Sugar

# $\mathcal{D}$irections:

1. Preheat oven to 300*F.  Spread pecans out on cookie sheet. Toast in preheated oven for 10 minutes.  Scoop toasted pecans into a bowl and coat with 2-3 Tbsp pure maple syrup.  Stir well. Set aside and raise oven temperature to 350*F.
2. Place first amount of water and ground flaxseed in a saucepan. Bring to a boil and simmer until thick, approximately 5 minutes. Set aside to cool.
3. Pour first amount of maple syrup, dates, extracts, salt, 1/3 cup water and cornstarch into a blender.  Add flax seed mixture and blend until smooth.
4. Prepare pie crust according to recipe instructions or package directions (depending if you choose to make your own crust from scratch or use *The Mix Company*'s prepackaged mix). Spray two 12-cup muffin pans with gluten free cooking spray to ensure your tarts will easily slide out later.
5. Roll out dough between two sheets of waxed paper.  Remove the top sheet and cut 24 circles to desired tart size.  A large-mouth mason jar ring works great.
6. Gently place each pastry circle into the muffin tin and lightly press down to form to the pastry to the shape of the cavity.  Fill each shell ¾ full with filling.
7. Bake in preheat oven for 15 minutes.  Remove from oven, top with a few maple-coated pecans and return to the oven for 15-20 minutes more or until firm and pecans are very lightly browned.
8. Cool completely before removing from pan.

# Baby or Bridal Shower

Lettuce Wraps with Eggless "Egg" Salad and
Chick Pea Tuna Salad
Hummus
Zucchini Relish
Summer Tomato Salad
Lentil Salad
Curried Rice Salad
Blueberry Cream Trifle

"Every good gift and every perfect gift is from above and cometh down from the Father of lights, with whom is no variableness, neither shadow of turning."

*James 1:17*

# Baby & Bridal Showers

Ok – I admit it. I'm a planaholic! I love everything to do with organizing, planning and hosting fun events like baby and bridal showers. The cute invitations, pretty decorations and unique party favors can all make the event fun and memorable. Another thing that you want the guests talking about for a while is how good the food was! In this section, I've included some of my favorite things to serve at a party – and what better way to make your guests feel like you've thought of every detail than to have options that suit a variety of food allergies and choices! You can confidently tell your guests that the entire menu is 100% gluten, dairy, egg and meat free!

# Lettuce Wraps

Using lettuce as an alternative to wraps is not only delicious, but it's a great way to cut down on your carbs and sodium and to add some green leafy vegetables to your diet!

To make lettuce wraps, simply take a large lettuce or other green leaf (such as romaine, leaf lettuce, collards, spinach, kale or swiss chard), fill it with approximately 2-3 Tbsp of your choice of filling (such as Eggless "Egg Salad" or Chick Pea Tuna Salad in this section), roll it up and secure it with a toothpick. Place on a serving platter and keep refrigerated until ready to serve. Simple and delicious!

# Eggless "Egg" Salad

This is pretty close to the real thing! I've included this recipe from my first cookbook because it is just a great staple in our house and anytime we want a good sandwich or wrap, the children are always requesting Eggless "Egg Salad)

Makes 4 cups

## Ingredients:

- 1-420g package of firm tofu, drained and rinsed
- ½ cup chopped celery
- 1 onion, minced
- ¼ cup Zucchini Relish, see recipe in this section
- 1 Tbsp chicken-style seasoning, (See *Seasonings and Extras*)
- 1 tsp turmeric
- ½ tsp garlic powder
- ¾ cup Creamy Garlic Spread, (See *Backyard Barbecue* Section)

## Directions:

1. Crumble tofu into a medium bowl. Add remaining ingredients and mix well. Store in an airtight container in the fridge.

## {Special Notes}

- Although this tastes best the same day it is made, it still is great as leftovers the next day and keeps well for 4-5 days.
- It's normal for separation to occur. Simply stir mixture before using.

# Chick Pea Tuna Salad

Chickpeas are known throughout the world by many different names including garbanzo beans, ceci (pronounced she-she) beans, chana, sanagalu, Gonzo Beans and Bengal gram.  Whichever name you know them by, they are delicious in this sandwich spread which is reminiscent of a tuna salad sandwich – without the cholesterol or risk of mercury consumption.

Makes approx. 2 cups

## Ingredients:

- 1 ½ cups cooked chickpeas (or 1-15 oz can)
- 1/4-1/2 cup Creamy Garlic Spread (See *Backyard Barbecue* Section)
- 1/3 cup minced celery
- 1 Tbsp Zucchini relish, see recipe in this section
- ½ Tbsp nutritional yeast
- 1-2 green onions, chopped
- 1 tbsp gluten free soy sauce
- Vegetable salt to taste

## Directions:

1. In a medium bowl, mash the chick peas with a potato masher. Mix in remaining ingredients and serve on gluten free bread or toast, gluten free wraps or wrap it up in large romaine lettuce leaves.  Great topped with lettuce or spinach and accompanied by Lemony Dill Pickles on the side!

# Hummus

I've included this recipe from my first cookbook because it's such a favorite and a stand-by for parties, picnics and road trips.   It's naturally gluten free and makes a great dip, spread or sandwich addition.

Makes 3 cups

- 1 19-oz can chickpeas OR 2 cups soaked and cooked chickpeas
- ½ cup water plus additional water for blending
- ¼ cup lemon juice
- 1/3 cup tahini (sesame paste, NOT sesame butter)
- 2 tsp garlic powder
- 1 tsp onion powder
- 2-3 Tbsp chopped fresh dill or1 tsp dried dill weed
- 1 tsp sea salt

1. Place all ingredients in a blender.  Blend on medium or high speed, depending on your blender.  Stop the blender to scrape down the sides and stir.  Add enough extra water a tablespoon at a time, if necessary, to achieve a creamy consistency.
2. Store in an airtight container in the refrigerator.

# Zucchini Relish

This recipe is from my first book but I use it in so many things, I just had to include it in here as well!

Makes approximately 20-25 250mL jars

## Ingredients:

- 1 ½ cups water
- 6 cups chopped onion
- 3 cups EACH chopped red pepper and chopped cauliflower
- 3 Tbsp salt
- 1 ½ cups honey
- 1 ½ tsp turmeric
- 1 ½ cups lemon juice
- 1 ½ tsp celery seed
- ½ tsp coriander
- ½ tsp rosemary
- 18 cups chopped zucchini
- ¾ cup arrowroot starch mixed with 1 ½ cups water

## Directions:

1. In a large pot, sauté onions and red pepper in a little water. Add cauliflower and seasonings and mix well.
2. Add honey and zucchini. Bring to a boil and cook over medium heat. When vegetables are tender yet firm, add flour and water. Continue cooking until thick.
3. Remove from heat and ladle into hot, sterilized 250 mL glass jars. Process for 15 minutes in a boiling water bath to ensure against spoilage.

# {Special Notes}

- This recipe makes a LOT so feel free to reduce by half or even ¾.
- Because it is sweetened with honey and not sugar, this relish only lasts a few days in the fridge once it's opened. It's best to use smaller jars rather than larger ones.

# Summer Tomato Salad

Nothing says summer like fresh tomatoes out of the garden!  Heirloom grape and cherry tomatoes make this salad extra special but if you don't have those, feel free to use whatever is in your garden.

Makes 6 servings

## Ingredients:

- 1 pint heirloom cherry tomatoes, quartered
- 1 pint heirloom grape or pear tomatoes, halved (yellow or purple are especially nice)
- ¼ cup chopped green onions
- 2 cloves garlic, minced
- ¼ cup chopped fresh basil
- 2 Tbsp finely chopped cilantro
- ½ tsp salt or to taste

## Directions:

1. Mix all ingredients together in a bowl and toss gently to combine.  Chill for 30 minutes or longer, toss again and serve.

# French Lentil Salad

We love this salad! It's so versatile – serve it hot, cold or at room temperature. It can also be used as a side or main dish. It travels well for potlucks or lunch at work and requires only a few ingredients.

Makes 10-12 servings

## Ingredients:

- 12 oz French lentils (smaller than green lentils)
- 3 garlic cloves, slightly smashed with the flat side of a large knife
- 1 clove garlic, minced (additional amount)
- 1 tsp salt
- ½ cup cold-pressed extra virgin olive oil
- Zest and juice from 1 lemon (approximately 3 Tbsp juice)
- 2 medium or 1 large carrot, peeled and finely diced

## Directions:

1. Place lentils and smashed garlic into a medium pot. Add enough water to cover by 2 inches, cover pot and bring to a boil over high heat. Reduce heat to medium-low and simmer for 10 minutes. Add salt, stir and simmer for 10 more minutes.
2. Turn off heat and let lentils sit for 15 minutes. Drain. At this point, you can either discard the garlic or you can mash it and stir it in to the lentils.
3. Pour drained lentils into a medium bowl and let cool. Add remaining ingredients and season with salt. If serving cold, chill for several hours.

## {Special Notes}

- French lentils are smaller than green lentils and require less water when cooking. They also retain their shape and firmness better than green lentils making them ideal for this salad.

# Curried Rice Salad

We love curry and rice and this salad makes for a lovely combination of the two flavors. Brown rice varieties are becoming more and more available and you can add a little extra flair to your dishes by incorporating choices like brown jasmine or basmati in.

Makes approximately 6 cups

## Ingredients:

- 4 cups cooked brown rice, jasmine or basmati are nice in this salad
- ½ English cucumber, diced
- ½ cup chopped onion
- 1 large carrot, shredded
- 1 tbsp minced fresh parsley
- 3 tbsp Creamy Garlic Spread (or more if you like it creamier) (See *Backyard Barbecue* Section)
- 2 tbsp canola oil or oil of your choice
- 1 tbsp lemon juice
- 2 tsp honey
- 1 tsp curry powder substitute (See *Seasonings and Extras*)
- 2 garlic cloves, minced
- 1 tsp salt
- ½ -1 pint cherry or grape tomatoes, halved (depending on how many tomatoes you like)

*D*irections:

1. In a large bowl, combine the first five ingredients. In another bowl, whisk together Creamy Garlic Spread, oil, lemon juice, honey, curry powder substitute, garlic and salt.
2. Stir into rice mixture. Just before serving, garnish with tomatoes.

# Blueberry Cream Trifle

I'll be the first to admit that this isn't the healthiest dessert you'll find but I think that sometimes it's ok to indulge a little!

Makes 1 trifle

## Ingredients:

- ½ recipe of Orange Delight Cupcakes (See *Happy Birthday* section), baked as an 8" or 9" square cake
- 1 can blueberry pie filling
- 1 package Kraft Fat Free/Sugar Free White Chocolate instant pudding
- 2 cartons NutriWhip non-dairy whipped topping
- Fresh blueberries and candied oranges for garnish, optional

## Directions:

1. Prepare ½ recipe for the cake according to recipe for Orange Delight Cupcakes. Pour batter into a greased 8" or 9" cake pan. Bake cake at 350* for approximately 25-30 minutes or until toothpick inserted in middle comes out clean.
2. Once cake is baked, set aside to cool. Once cooled, cut into ½" cubes.
3. In a large mixing bowl, whip up 1 carton of Nutriwhip. Set aside.
4. In another large bowl, combine second package of Nutriwhip with the package of instant pudding. Whip for several minutes or until semi-firm.

5. In a trifle bowl or large clear glass bowl, place a layer of cake cubes. Spoon on a layer of blueberry pie filling and then a layer of pudding/cream mixture. Add another layer of cake and then a layer of plain Nutriwhip. Repeat this pattern, reserving the final layer of plain Nutriwhip for the top.
6. Garnish with blueberries and candied oranges if desired.

*Notes:*

# Backyard Barbecue

Barbecue Sauce
Potato Salad
Salsa Skillet Pasta
Lemony Dill Pickles
Black Bean Burgers
Creamy Garlic Spread
Avocado Key Lime Pie

Life in the open air is good for body and mind. It is God's medicine for the restoration of health.

E. G. White

# Mmmm.....Barbecues!

T-bone steaks, hamburgers, hotdogs, salmon steaks, sausages....these are among the typical items that you would usually find on a grill in the summer time.  So what is one to do when you've made the decision to follow a plant-based diet?  Are barbecues and backyard get-togethers a thing of the past?  I'm here to tell you that they don't have to be!

It's not impossible to have a delicious and healthy meal without all the fat, cholesterol and sugar that usually accompanies outdoor cooking.  In this section, you'll find some of our favorite summertime meals – and they're kid tested and approved, too!

# Barbecue Sauce

The perfect topping for Black Bean Burgers! This is a great recipe because there are no refined sugars and irritating vinegar like the commercial varieties have.

Makes 3 ½ cups

## Ingredients:

- 3 cups tomato puree (1-5.5 oz/156mL can tomato paste mixed with enough water to equal 3 cups)
- 5 tbsp blackstrap or fancy molasses
- ½ cup honey
- 2 tsp onion powder
- 1 Tbsp garlic powder
- ½ Tbsp parsley flakes
- 3 tbsp gluten free soy sauce
- 2 tbsp lemon juice

## Directions:

1. Place all ingredients in a saucepan. Bring to a boil, reduce heat and simmer for 10 minutes

## {Special Notes}

- Tomato sauce is generally made from less-than-acceptable tomatoes and quite often is loaded with salt and sugar to give it a better flavor. Tomato paste, on the other hand, is made with top quality tomatoes. As a general rule of thumb, you can make your own tomato sauce by combining 1 5.5oz can with 2 cups water.

# Potato Salad

You can't have a barbecue without potato salad! We enjoy this side dish so much that I just had to include it in both cookbooks.

Makes 12 large servings

## Ingredients:

- 3 lbs potatoes, peeled and cut into chunks
- 2 stalks celery, diced
- 1 medium onion, minced
- ½ - 2/3 cup Lemony Dill Pickles
- ½ tsp garlic powder
- 1/3 tsp turmeric
- 2 Tbsp Chicken-style seasoning ((see *Seasonings and Extras*)
- 3 Tbsp Nutritional yeast
- 1 tsp onion powder
- 2 ½ cups Creamy Garlic Spread

## Directions:

1. Several hours before serving, prepare potatoes. Peel and cut potatoes, place in a large pot, cover with water, bring to a boil and simmer, covered, until tender – about 15-17 minutes.
2. Drain potatoes, mash and transfer to a large serving bowl. Refrigerate for a few hours or until cool.
3. Meanwhile, chop celery, onions and pickles. Place in bowl with cooled potatoes.
4. Add seasonings and Creamy Garlic Spread. Mix well and chill until ready to serve. If preparing in advance, you may need to add a bit more Creamy Garlic Spread before serving depending on how creamy you like your potato salad.

# Salsa Skillet Pasta

This skillet meal can easily be prepared on the side-burner of your bbq or inside the house on the stovetop. Simple, quick and delicious!

Makes 6-8 servings

## Ingredients:

- 2 cups uncooked gluten free pasta (Fusilli is a nice choice)
- 1 onion, chopped
- 3 cloves garlic, minced
- 1 large green pepper, chopped or julienned
- 1 small can (approximately 1 cup) corn (frozen corn can be used as well)
- 1 – 1 ½ cups black beans, rinsed
- 1 ¼ cups salsa (or enough to keep the pasta moist)
- 1 cup Daiya mozzarella-style shreds, optional

## Directions:

1. In a large saucepan, boil water. Add pasta, stir, cover and turn off heat. Let sit in hot water for 8-12 minutes or until desired texture is reached. Rinse with cold water, return to the pot, cover and set aside.
2. In a large skillet, sauté onion, garlic and peppers in a little water until tender. Add corn, beans, pasta and salsa and gently stir. Heat through. Top with shredded mozzarella-style cheese if desired and keep on low heat for a few minutes more until the cheese has had a chance to melt slightly.

# Lemony Dill Pickles

Not only are these a delicious addition to Potato Salad, they make a great burger topper!

Makes 1-1L jar

## Ingredients:
- ½ cup lemon juice, fresh or bottled
- 2 Tbsp salt
- 2-3 cloves garlic, sliced
- 1 tsp dried dill
- 1 large English cucumber
- 1L glass jar with lid (a large canning jar works perfectly)

## Directions:
1. Fill glass jar with lemon juice, salt, garlic and dill.
2. Slice cucumbers into rounds. Fill jar with cucumber slices. Fill jar with water and cover with lid. Shake briefly to combine all ingredients.
3. Put in refrigerator and let sit for 24 hours. These will keep in the fridge for at least 2 weeks. They never last in our house that long though!

## {Special Notes}
- We use these pickles as a great alternative to the traditional vinegar-brined dill pickles. Vinegar increases our body's acidity which makes us more prone to disease and illness. Vinegar also decreases the blood clotting factor in our blood. Family favorites like these pickles can still be enjoyed with the addition of lemon juice instead of vinegar.

# Black Bean Burgers

If you're looking for a delicious burger, look no further! These are cholesterol free, extremely low in fat, and barbecue well! Grab your favorite toppings and enjoy this great summertime meal.

Makes 10-12 burgers

## Ingredients:

- 1 medium onion, quartered
- 2 jalapenos, halved and seeds removed OR 2/3 tsp jalapeno powder
- 6 garlic cloves, peeled
- 2 19-oz cans black beans, drained and rinsed
- 1 ¼ cups wheat free quick oats
- 1 large can corn, optional (if you have a corn allergy, you can leave this ingredient out)
- 4 tsp cumin
- 1 tsp curry powder substitute (See *Seasonings and Extras*)
- ¼ cup salsa
- 1 tsp salt
- ½ cup ground oats, only as needed
- Barbecue sauce

## Directions:

1. Place1 ¼ cups oats in food processor. Process until ground. Pour into a large bowl. Add cumin, curry powder and salt, stir to combine and set aside.
2. Place onion, jalapenos and garlic in a food processor and pulse a few times or until pieces are about as small as a pencil eraser. Scrape into bowl with ground oats.

3. Once again in the food processor, place black beans and optional corn. Pulse 4-5 times, scrape down sides and pulse an additional 4-5 times. If your food processor is small or less powerful, you may have to do this in two batches. Pour into bowl with onion and oat mixture, add salsa and mix well.
4. Cover with plastic wrap and leave in refrigerator for at least two hours but can be left in for longer than that.
5. Remove chilled mixture from refrigerator. If the mixture is too sticky to be formed into firm, well shaped patties, add enough ground oats to make it a good consistency (add a small amount at a time).
6. Form into patties and gently place on an oiled grill. Barbecue for 6-8 minutes per side or until patties have reached desired doneness. Flip patties, baste with barbecue sauce and cook for an additional 6-8 minutes, checking often for doneness.
7. Serve alone or on a toasted gluten free hamburger bun with toppings of your choice.

# {Special Notes}

- Although traditional toppings like ketchup, mustard and relish are usually the first to be chosen, why not try something different on your burger? Some good suggestions are sprouts, guacamole, Daiya cheese slices, caramelized onions and mushrooms or Creamy Garlic Spread.

# Creamy Garlic Spread

We use this in place of mayonnaise in many recipes. It works wonderfully in Potato Salad, as a spread on sandwiches or as a base for creamy dips.

Makes 2 cups

## Ingredients:
- ½ cup sunflower seeds
- ½ cup water
- 1-17.5 oz package of silken tofu
- 3 ½ Tbsp lemon juice
- 1 tsp salt
- 1 tsp garlic powder
- 1 ½ tsp onion powder

## Directions:
1. Place all ingredients in a blender and blend until smooth. Will thicken as it chills.

## {Special Notes}
- Soaking the sunflower seeds in water for a few hours beforehand will help them blend up more smoothly and make them more easily digested.
- This will keep for approximately 1 week in the refrigerator.

# Avocado Key Lime Pie

Cool, creamy and delicious describes this pie that is a perfect end to a great summer meal.

## Ingredients:

### Crust:
- 1 cup unsweetened, shredded coconut
- 1 cup walnuts
- 8-10 dates
- Water, as needed
- Pinch of salt

### Directions:
1. Place the coconut, walnuts and salt in a food processor. Pulse 5-7 times.
2. Add dates one at a time and process until the mixture starts to come together. Add a little water (1-2 tsp) if needed to hold together. Press into the bottom of a 9-inch pie plate and place in freezer while you prepare the filling.

### Filling:
- 3 avocados
- ½-3/4 cup lime juice
- Zest of 1 lime, optional
- 1 cup raw, unsalted cashews, soaked for 4-6 hours and drained
- 1/4 cup coconut oil, warmed
- 1/2 cup maple syrup
- 2 tsp pure vanilla extract

- ¼ tsp sea salt

# Directions:

1. Place all filling ingredients into blender and blend until smooth and creamy.
2. Pour filling into prepared crust and chill in the freezer for 3-4 hours. Take out of freezer 10-15 minutes before serving.

# {Special Notes}

- An avocado is ripe when the skin turns from a green color to a dark brown or almost black color. You will also be able to press the sides in ever so slightly. To speed the ripening process, place avocados in a brown paper bag with a banana, apple or tomato. Close the bag and leave at room temperature. The avocados should ripen in 1-3 days.
- Did you know that avocados are great for pregnant women? They're also the same shape of the uterus and interestingly, it takes 9 months for an avocado to be ready!

# Brunch

Blueberry Muffins (with variations)
Cranberry Banana Muffins
Oatmeal Raisin Scones
Fruit Kebabs
Peach Strawberry Banana Smoothie
Banana Blueberry Pancakes

"Brunch is cheerful, sociable and inciting.  It is talk-compelling. It puts you in a good temper, it makes you satisfied with yourself and your fellow beings; it sweeps away the worries and cobwebs of the week."

*Guy Beringer*

# Brunch

There have been many times that I've stayed at a hotel that offers a "free continental breakfast" – which usually translates into a light brunch that includes a whole lot of things that are off limits for a gluten free vegan!  Why not host a brunch for you and your friends where you can be in control of the menu and be sure to have something for everyone to enjoy!

# Blueberry Muffins

We really enjoy having fresh-baked muffins for breakfast, or in this case, brunch! It's easy to whip up a batch of these muffins in the morning and pop them in the oven. In less than an hour, you'll be enjoying delicious, hot-out-of-the-oven muffins!

Makes 14-16 muffins

## Ingredients:
- 1 cup sorghum flour
- 1 cup rice flour
- ½ cup tapioca starch
- 2 tbsp potato starch
- 1 tsp xanthan gum
- 2 tsp baking powder
- 1 tsp baking soda
- ½ tsp salt
- ¼ tsp cardamom
- ¼ tsp coriander
- ¾ cup orange juice
- ½ cup unsweetened applesauce
- ½ cup maple syrup or Sucanat
- ½ cup vegetable oil or warmed and liquefied coconut oil
- 2 tsp pure vanilla extract
- 1 tsp orange extract
- 3 cups fresh or frozen blueberries

## Directions:
1. Preheat oven to 350*F. Spray muffin cups and set aside.

2. In a large bowl, combine the flours, baking powder, baking soda, salt, cardamom and coriander. Mix well.
3. In a 4-cup measuring cup, mix together orange juice, applesauce, sweetener, oil, and extracts. Pour the wet ingredients into the dry and mix together well.
4. Add the blueberries and mix well.
5. Spoon batter into muffin cups. Bake in preheated oven for 20-25 minutes.

# {Special Notes}

Variations:
- Rhubarb Muffins: Replace blueberries with an equal amount of fresh, diced rhubarb
- Berry Blast Muffins: Replace blueberries with an equal amount of mixed berries, fresh or frozen. Fill muffin cups 1/3 full, place 1 tsp any flavored jam on top of batter (strawberry or blueberry is nice), and spoon on remaining batter. Bake as usual.
- Rhubarb Cake: Replace blueberries with an equal amount of fresh, diced rhubarb. Spoon batter into a greased 9x13 glass baking dish, top with maple syrup-coated pecans and bake for 30-35 minutes in preheated 350*F oven.

# Cranberry Banana Muffins

As I was wishing one day for a warm banana muffin right out of the oven just like my mom used to make, it occurred to me that I had her recipe and all I had to do was add a gluten free and vegan spin to it for my wish to come true. This is the result – a moist, flavorful muffin that has no gluten, dairy, egg or refined sugar. I hope you enjoy it as much as we do!

Makes 12 muffins

## Ingredients:

- 3 large bananas (about 1 ½ cups)
- 2/3 cup maple syrup
- 1 ½ Tbsp ground flax mixed with ¼ cup warm water
- 1 tsp baking powder
- 1 tsp baking soda
- ½ tsp salt
- ½ cup brown rice flour
- ½ cup sorghum flour
- ½ cup tapioca starch
- ¾ tsp xanthan gum
- ¾ tsp pure vanilla extract
- 1/3 cup vegetable or liquefied coconut oil
- 1 cup coarsely chopped cranberries, fresh or frozen
- ¼ tsp EACH cardamom and coriander

## Directions:

1. Preheat oven to 375*F. Mix ground flax with water and set aside for 10 minutes.

2. Mash bananas and place in a large mixing bowl.  Add syrup, flax seed mixture and oil.  Stir well.
3. Add the remaining ingredients and stir well to combine.
4. Spray a 12-cup muffin pan with non-stick spray.  Divide batter evenly among the 12 cups.
5. Bake in preheated oven for 20-25 minutes or until toothpick inserted in the middle of a muffin comes out clean.
6. Cool in pan for 10-15 minutes before removing to a wire rack to cool completely.

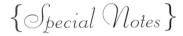 {Special Notes}

Variations:
- Replace cranberries with ½ cup carob chips, 1 cup chopped walnuts or 1 cup frozen or fresh blueberries and omit the cardamom and coriander.  Bake as usual.

# Oatmeal Raisin Scones

The first time I made these scones, I was very pleased at the outcome. The millet flour, sorghum flour and grated apple help to keep them moist and the cardamom and coriander complement the apple and raisins nicely. While, like most gluten free baking, they are best eaten fresh out of the oven, they also reheat well the next day. Enjoy with a little vegan butter and homemade strawberry jam for a delicious addition to your breakfast or brunch.

Makes 12 scones

## Ingredients:

- 1 cup + 2 Tbsp soy or other non-dairy milk
- 1 Tbsp lemon juice
- 1 cup sorghum flour
- ½ cup brown rice flour
- ½ cup gluten free millet flour ("Purest" brand is our favorite)
- 1 1/2 Tbsp baking powder
- ¾ tsp xanthan gum
- 1/4 cup cane sugar
- ¼ tsp salt
- 1/8 tsp cardamom
- 1/8 tsp coriander
- 1 ¼ cups wheat free large flake oats
- 1/3 cup all-vegetable shortening
- ½ cup raisins
- ½ cup peeled, grated apple
- 1 tsp maple extract
- 2 Tbsp soy or other non-dairy milk (additional amount)

## $\mathcal{D}$irections:

1. In a 2-cup measuring cup, mix the non-dairy milk and lemon juice together. Set aside to curdle.
2. Preheat oven to 400*F.
3. In a large mixing bowl, combine dry ingredients and stir to combine. Cut in shortening and mix together with a pastry blender until well blended and a meal-like consistency is obtained.
4. Add raisins and stir. Finally, add in the grated apple, maple extract and non-dairy milk. Mix well with a wooden spoon or sturdy spatula until a soft (but not sticky) dough forms.
5. Turn dough out onto large rice-flour dusted cutting board or countertop.
6. Divide the dough into two equal portions. Press together and form into two discs – about ½" in height. Using a sharp knife, cut each disc into 6 wedges. Place on parchment lined cookie sheet. Brush the top of each wedge with non-dairy milk and place in preheated oven.
7. Bake for 15-17 minutes or until golden brown on the top. Let cool for approximately 15-20 minutes so the scones have a chance to firm up. Serve warm with vegan butter, honey or jam.

## {$\mathcal{S}$pecial $\mathcal{N}$otes}

- Dried cranberries, cherries or blueberries can be substituted for the raisins

# Fruit Kebabs

What a fun way to serve fruit! Kids love eating their fruit off of a skewer and adults love the beautiful presentation that it offers.

## Ingredients:

- Fresh fruit such as strawberries, apples, pineapple, grapes, starfruit, oranges, kiwi, bananas or pears
- Wooden or stainless steel skewers

## Directions:

1. Wash, peel and core if necessary and cut fruit into bite sized chunks. Leave grapes and strawberries whole.
2. Slide one piece of each fruit onto each skewer, leaving a 1-inch space at the end of each skewer.
3. Place on a serving platter and keep refrigerated until ready to serve.

## {Special Notes}

- Keep in mind – if you decide to use fruits that brown quickly after being cut, such as apples or pears, you may want to assemble the kebabs just before serving to avoid having an off-color to your beautiful presentation!

# Peach Strawberry Banana Smoothie

Using fresh peaches and strawberries makes this smoothie extra nice but frozen will work well too. Add some fresh greens like spinach or kale for an added nutritional punch!

Makes 5 cups

## Ingredients:

- 2 large or 3 medium peaches, peeled and sliced
- 2 cups fresh or frozen strawberries
- 1 or 2 frozen bananas, cut in chunks
- 1 cup orange juice

## Directions:

1. Place all ingredients in a blender and blend until smooth. Add a little water if needed to achieve your desired texture and thickness.

# Banana Blueberry Pancakes

These are one of our favorite breakfast items! They're so filling and hearty - loaded with antioxidant-rich blueberries, potassium-packed bananas and high-fibre oats, these pancakes are sure to keep you going for hours!

Makes 12-15 pancakes

## Ingredients:

- 2 cups almond milk or other non-dairy milk
- 1 Tbsp lemon juice
- 2 ½ cups wheat-free large-flake oats
- ½ cup sorghum flour
- ½ cup brown rice flour
- ½ cup buckwheat flour
- 2 tsp baking powder
- ½ tsp salt
- 1 apple, diced
- 1-2 cups fresh or frozen blueberries
- 1 banana, mashed
- ¼ cup unsweetened applesauce
- 3/4 cup water
- 1 Tbsp liquefied coconut oil OR vegetable oil

## Directions:

1. In a 4-cup measuring cup, combine the almond milk and lemon juice.  Set aside for about 5 minutes.
2. In a large bowl, combine oats, flours, baking powder, salt, apple, blueberries and banana.

3. Add applesauce and oil to almond milk mixture. Stir to combine and then add to dry ingredients. Add water.
4. Stir well and let sit for 15-20 minutes. This helps the large flake oats to absorb more liquid, be softer and easier to digest. You may need to add a bit of water to give you the desired consistency after the batter has sat.
5. Heat a griddle over medium-high heat. Add a tablespoon of coconut oil and allow to heat through. Spoon batter onto griddle and cook until slightly bubbly, about 4 minutes. Flip and cook for another 4-5 minutes or until done.
6. Serve with pure maple syrup or applesauce mixed with jam. Also great with peanut butter or peaches.

## {Special Notes}

- Another way to serve these pancakes is to "stuff" them with jam. Simply pour a small amount of batter on your preheated pan (about ¼ cup), top with 1 Tbsp of your favorite jam and then add another 1/3 cup or so of batter on top of that. This will create a delicious jam filling and will be a fun surprise for the children!

# Games Night

Potato Skins
Pizza Popcorn
Guacamole
Hot Broccoli & Mushroom Dip
Mexican Pie
Peppermint Patty Brownies

"There is nothing in the world so irresistibly contagious as laughter and good humor."

*Charles Dickens*

# Games Night

Isn't it fun to have an evening filled with laughter and camaraderie while playing some games and getting to know your friends and family better?  What are your favorite board games to play?  Try to plan a night where you get together with your friends, family or neighbors for a fun-filled time.  All the menu planning is already done for you on the next few pages so all you have to do is send the invitations out and have a good time!

# Potato Skins

Potatoes in any form are a favorite around our house. I hadn't had potato skins for years and decided one day I wanted to make some! The result was a delicious and healthy appetizer or party food that's sure to be a crowd pleaser.

Makes 24 pieces

## Ingredients:

- 6 medium baking potatoes
- ½ recipe Cheeze Sauce (see *Movie Night* section), increasing the rice flour to 6 Tbsp per ½ batch (you want the cheese sauce thicker for the potato skins) OR 1 pkg Daiya cheddar-style shreds
- 2 green onions, chopped
- Gluten free meatless bacon bits
- 1 recipe Sunflower Sour Cream (see *Movie Night* section)

## Directions:

1. Wash potatoes and prick with a fork a few times. Place on a cookie sheet and bake for approximately 1 hour at 350*F or until done. Set aside to cool.
2. Meanwhile, make ½ recipe of the Cheeze Sauce. Once it's thickened, set aside.
3. Once the potatoes are cool enough to handle, cut lengthwise in half and then cut each piece in half again. Scoop out most of the potato, leaving approximately ¼"-1/3" thick skin/potato. Place on baking sheet.
4. Preheat oven to 350*F.

5.  Spread ½ Tbsp thickened cheese sauce on each potato piece. Top with green onions and meatless bacon bits.
6.  Bake in preheated oven for 10 minutes.  Sprinkle with salt and serve with Sunflower Sour Cream.

# Pizza Popcorn

Baking popcorn adds a whole new dimension to its texture and flavor. This is one of our favorite snacks because it is so flavorful and quick to throw together.

Makes 10 cups

## Ingredients:

- 10 cups popped popcorn
- 1/3 cup non-hydrogenated vegan margarine (Vegan Becel or Earth Balance)
- ¼ cup Parmesan Cheeze Please *(See Extras and Seasonings)*
- ½ tsp garlic powder
- 1 tsp salt
- ½ tsp oregano
- ½ tsp basil
- ¼ tsp onion powder

## Directions:

1. Preheat oven to 350*F.
2. Place popcorn in an ungreased roasting pan. Melt margarine in a small saucepan and add remaining ingredients. Pour over popcorn and mix well.
3. Bake in preheated oven for 15 minutes.

# Guacamole

Avocados seem to be one of those foods that people either love or hate! I encourage you to try this dip even if you're not a fan of avocados. You may become one after tasting this delicious recipe!

## Ingredients:

- 3 ripe avocados
- ½ tsp onion powder or 1 green onion diced
- 1 clove garlic, pressed
- 1 tbsp lemon juice
- ½ tsp salt
- 1/3 cup finely diced tomato

1. Carefully cut avocados in half and remove pit. Scoop out flesh into a small bowl and mash with a fork.
2. Add remaining ingredients and mix well. Serve with corn chips or use as a layer in *Mexican Pie* (see recipe in this section)

## {Special Notes}

- Although avocados are a little high in natural fats and calories, they have a host of health benefits that you want to cash in on. They're full of disease-fighting antioxidants, are high in fibre, can help stabilize blood sugar, can help lower your cholesterol and are high in folate (great for pregnant women!)
- Avocados make an excellent replacement for margarine or mayonnaise on bread. Mix it with a little minced garlic and a sprinkle of salt for a delicious and healthy spread
- To keep leftover avocados from turning brown, lightly spray the flesh with cooking spray or brush with lemon juice and wrap in plastic wrap

# Hot Broccoli & Mushroom Dip

Warm and delicious describes this party dip that is sure to be a crowd pleaser!  Serve with gluten free corn chips or in a hollowed out gluten free/vegan pumpernickel loaf with bread cubes.

Makes 10-12 servings

## Ingredients:

- 4 cups fresh chopped broccoli (chopped in bite-sized pieces)
- 1 medium onion, chopped finely
- 1 can mushrooms, pieces or chopped, drained
- 2-3 cloves garlic, minced
- ½ cup sliced toasted almonds
- 1 1/3 cups water
- ¼ cup cashews
- 1 ½ tbsp tahini
- 2 tsp lemon juice
- 1 tsp salt
- 2 Tbsp nutritional yeast flakes
- ½ Tbsp onion powder
- ½ tsp garlic powder
- 1 ½ Tbsp brown rice flour

## Directions:

1. Steam the broccoli along with the chopped onion.  Set aside.
2. Place the water, cashews, tahini, lemon juice, salt, nutritional yeast, onion powder, garlic powder and rice flour in a blender

until smooth.  Pour into a large saucepan (need to account for the other ingredients that will be added) and heat over medium-high heat until thickened, stirring constantly with a whisk.

3. Add cooked broccoli and onion mixture, mushrooms and garlic and heat through.  Add toasted almonds just before serving.

# Mexican Pie

Do you remember the layered party dip that gained popularity years ago?  This delicious, all plant-based version will have your party guests coming back for more!

Makes 15 servings

## Ingredients:

- 2 cups of cooked pinto beans
- ½ cup diced tomatoes
- 2 tsp chili powder  substitute (see *Seasonings and Extras*)
- 2 cloves garlic, minced
- ½ tsp oregano
- 1/8 tsp jalapeno powder, optional
- 1 recipe Guacamole (see this section)
- 12 oz silken tofu
- 2 tbsp lemon juice
- ½ tsp salt
- ½ tsp onion powder
- 2 medium tomatoes, diced
- 3 green onions, thinly sliced
- 1 can sliced black olives
- 1 green pepper, chopped
- Shredded lettuce
- Daiya cheddar-style cheese shreds, optional
- Corn chips for dipping

# *D*irections:

1. Place beans, tomatoes, chili powder, garlic, oregano and jalapeno powder in a blender. Blend briefly (mixture will be slightly smooth and slightly chunky). Scoop out into 9x13 glass dish and spread over the bottom. Now is a good time to wash out your blender. You're going to need it again shortly.

2. Prepare Guacamole according to recipe directions. Spread on top of bean layer.

3. In blender, blend together tofu, lemon juice, salt, and onion powder until smooth. Pour over Guacamole layer and make level.

4. Layer the remaining ingredients, one at a time, in the pan. Finish with Daiya cheddar-style cheese shreds.

5. Chill for a couple of hours before serving. Serve with gluten free corn chips or gluten free pita chips.

# Peppermint Patty Brownies

Many years ago, my grandmother invented a delicious peppermint patty cake where she baked a chocolate cake and then while it was still warm, she placed round chocolate-covered peppermint patties on top. It was one of my favorite desserts growing up and this gluten free and vegan version certainly ranks up there with my granny's sweet treat!

Makes 1-8" square pan

## Ingredients:

- 1/2 cup cane sugar
- 1/4 cup sorghum flour
- 1/4 cup brown rice flour
- 1/4 cup potato starch
- 1/2 cup sifted carob powder
- 1/2 teaspoon baking powder
- 1/2 teaspoon xanthan gum
- 1/4 teaspoon salt
- 1/4 cup vegetable oil
- 1/2 cup soy or almond milk
- 1 teaspoon peppermint extract
- 2 Tablespoons non-hydrogenated vegan margarine
- heaping 3/4 cup gluten free icing sugar
- 1/8 teaspoon peppermint extract
- 1/2-1 Tablespoon water or non-dairy milk
- 3/4 cup carob chips
- 2 teaspoons all-vegetable shortening

- 1/8 teaspoon peppermint extract

## Directions:

1. Preheat oven to 350* F. Grease an 8" square pan or line with parchment paper.
2. In a medium bowl, mix together sugar, sorghum flour, rice flour, potato starch, carob powder, baking powder, xanthan gum and salt.
3. Add oil, non-dairy milk and peppermint extract and stir well to combine. Pour into prepared pan and smooth.
4. Bake for 16-18 minutes or until brownie is slightly starting to pull away from the edges of the pan.
5. Let cool completely (I put mine in the freezer for a couple of hours to speed up the process – after all, who wants to wait all day for mint brownies???)
6. Meanwhile, to make the peppermint cream filling: in a small bowl, combine margarine, most of the icing sugar and the peppermint extract with an electric mixer. Add 1/2 Tablespoon water and mix until fluffy. Add more sugar and/or water to achieve desired consistency. You want it to be thicker than buttercream but still be able to spread it.
7. Spoon on top of completely cooled brownies and spread evenly. Place in the freezer for 15 minutes.
8. For the carob topping: melt carob chips and shortening using a double boiler. Stir until completely melted. Remove from heat and mix in peppermint extract and pour over peppermint cream layer. Place in freezer for an hour or until carob layer is completely solid.
9. Store in the fridge or the freezer.  Refrigerates well for several days.

# Lunch with Friends

Cream of Cauliflower Soup
Curried Pumpkin Soup
Veggie Taco Salad
Multigrain Loaf
Strawberry Macaroon Bars

"I would rather walk with a friend in the dark, than alone in the light."
*Helen Keller*

# Lunch with Friends

What a great way to enjoy an afternoon – having lunch with good friends.  Simple meals like soups, salads and breads are always a favorite and make a hearty and warming lunch option.  Here's to food, friends, and great memories!

# Cream of Cauliflower Soup

Cashews are a wonderful way to add a rich, creamy flavor to soups that are traditionally made with cream or milk. This soup is so flavorful and delicious and goes perfectly with a slice of fresh bread and a salad.

Makes 8 servings

## Ingredients:

- 2 medium onions, chopped
- 3 garlic cloves, minced
- 1 1/2 cup diced celery
- 6 cups water, divided into 5 cups and 1 cup
- ½ head cauliflower, chopped into bite-sized pieces and steamed until tender
- 2-3 medium potatoes, cubed (optionally you can peel them)
- 3 Tbsp nutritional yeast
- 1 1/2 tsp Chicken style seasoning
- 1 1/2 tsp salt
- 3/4 cup unsalted cashews
- 1/3 cup brown rice flour

## Directions:

1. In a steamer, steam cauliflower until tender. Meanwhile, in a saucepan, sauté onion, garlic and celery in a little water until softened. Add potatoes, nutritional yeast, chicken-style seasoning and salt. Cover with approximately 5 cups water. Bring to a boil and simmer until potatoes are cooked.

2. Place cashews in a blender and blend with the 1 cup of water until very smooth and creamy. Add to potato mixture and stir well.

3. Combine brown rice flour with a small amount of water and mix well to get any lumps out. Stir into soup and cook until thickened. Gently stir cauliflower into thickened soup. Serve hot with fresh bread and a salad!

# Curried Pumpkin Soup

This mild-flavored soup is a great way to use up some of the extra pumpkin that many of us are blessed with in the fall months. This is a favorite among children as well.

Serves 4-6

## Ingredients:

- 1 medium onion, chopped
- 2 stalks celery, chopped
- 2 medium carrots, chopped
- 3 medium potatoes, cubed
- 3 cups cooked and pureed pumpkin
- 4 cups water mixed with 2 Tbsp Chicken-style seasoning (See *Seasonings and Extras)*
- 1 Tbsp curry powder
- Salt to taste

## Directions:

1. In large pot, sauté onion, celery and carrots in a small amount of water over medium heat for approximately 5 minutes.
2. Add remaining ingredients to the pot and bring to a boil. Reduce heat, cover and simmer for 40 minutes or until all vegetables are tender, stirring occasionally.
3. Pour soup in small batches into a blender and blend until smooth. Pour into another pot or soup tureen. Alternatively, you can blend it right in the pot with a handheld blender.

## {Special Notes}

- This soup also cans well. To pressure can, pour HOT soup into hot sterilized 1-quart jars. Add lid and ring and process for 80 minutes at 10 lbs pressure. Refer to your pressure canner's instruction manual for full details on how to safely pressure can.

# Veggie Taco Salad

This salad makes a delicious meal. It's really great on a hot summer day when you don't feel like cooking or it can also goes well alongside soup and bread.

## Dressing: (makes 3 cups)

- ½ cup raw, unsalted sunflower seeds
- ½ cup tahini (sesame seed paste)
- 2 tsp onion powder
- 1 ½ tsp salt
- 1 ¼ cups water
- ½ cup lemon juice, fresh if possible but bottled works well too
- 2-3 cloves garlic
- 1 tsp dill weed
- 1 Tbsp dried parsley flakes

1. Place all ingredients into a blender and blend until smooth.

## Salad:

- 6 cups romaine or leaf lettuce, cut into bite-sized pieces
- 1-2 avocadoes, peeled, pit removed and sliced
- 1 can or 2 cups cooked black beans, drained and rinsed
- 1 small can corn, drained
- 2 cups halved grape tomatoes
- 1 English cucumber, diced
- ½ cup red onion, finely chopped
- 1 cup Daiya cheddar-style shreds, optional
- 1 cup salsa
- 1 cup Dill Dressing (see above)

1. Layer all ingredients in the order given except salsa and dressing.
2. Combine salsa and dressing. Allow guests to pour desired amount over each serving. Serve with gluten free corn chips.

# Multigrain Loaf

This loaf is full of whole grain goodness!

Makes 1 medium loaf

## Ingredients:

- 2 Tbsp whole chia seeds
- ½ cup water
- 2 ¼ tsp instant yeast
- 1 cup warm water
- 2 Tbsp cane sugar
- ½ cup buckwheat flour
- 1 cup tapioca starch
- ½ cup chick pea flour
- ½ cup gluten free millet flour
- 1 tsp salt
- 1 tsp xanthan gum
- 3 Tbsp olive oil

## Directions:

1. In a small bowl, combine the chia seeds and ½ cup water. Let sit for 15 minutes.
2. In a 2-cup measuring cup, place warm water and cane sugar. Dissolve sugar in water and then add the yeast. Gently stir the yeast in and set aside to proof, about 10 minutes.
3. Preheat oven to 450*F. In a glass baking dish, place 1 inch of water. Place this pan on the bottom rack in the oven (this acts

as a hot water bath to add moisture to the oven while the bread is baking)

4. In a large mixing bowl, combine dry ingredients. Add the soaked chia seeds, yeast mixture and olive oil. Stir well until combined (dough will be slightly sticky).

5. Turn out onto countertop that has been generously dusted with brown rice flour.

6. Knead dough a few times and then gently form into a loaf that's approximately 8" long and 1 ¼" tall. Place formed dough onto parchment-covered cookie sheet. Score with a line that runs slightly off-centre.

7. Reduce oven to 375*F and bake for an hour. Turn oven off and leave in for 20 minutes. Cool before slicing.

# Strawberry Macaroon Bars

If you like coconut, than this recipe is for you! Feel free to use whatever flavor of jam you like, but our favorite is strawberry.

Makes 9x13 pan

## Ingredients:

### Crust:

- 2 ½ cups unsweetened coconut
- ½ cup brown rice flour
- ½ cup sorghum flour
- ¼ cup tapioca starch
- ¼ cup almond meal (or grind almonds in food processor )
- ¼ tsp salt
- ½ cup non-dairy milk
- ½ cup pure maple syrup
- ¼ cup coconut oil or vegetable oil
- ½ tsp pure vanilla extract

### Filling:

- 3 ½ - 4 cups jam, naturally sweetened if possible

### Topping:

- 1 cup unsweetened coconut

- ¼ cup sorghum flour
- ¼ cup brown rice flour
- 3 Tbsp liquefied coconut oil or vegetable oil
- ¼ tsp salt

1. Preheat oven to 350*F.
2. In a medium bowl, combine all ingredients for crust.  Press in a 9x13 glass baking dish that has been sprayed or lined with parchment paper.
3. Spread jam over top and smooth.
4. Prepare topping by mixing topping ingredients together in a small bowl.  Sprinkle evenly over top of jam layer.  Bake in preheated oven for 28-30 minutes.  Cool completely and cut into bars.

# {Special Notes}

Fun Coconut Facts!:
- Coconut trees can grow up to 30 meters tall!
- Besides culinary uses, coconuts are used for cosmetic purposes and for repelling mosquitoes
- Every bit of the coconut tree is used and has therefore gained the name "The Tree of Life" – from drinks to food to fuel to utensils and more
- Coconut water is identical to human plasma.  During the Pacific War of 1941-1945, coconut water was used to give emergency plasma transfusions to wounded soldiers.  Coconut water was also used as an IV drip in WWII.

# Romantic Dinner For Two

Zesty Kale Salad
Garlic Bread
Veggie Pasta Sauce
Sweetheart Brownies for Two

"Eve was created from a rib taken from the side of Adam, signifying that she was not to control him as the head, nor to be trampled under his feet as an inferior, but to stand by his side as an equal, to be loved and protected by him."

*E.G. White*

# Romantic Dinner for Two

It's date night – and you weren't able to find a sitter.  What is one to do?  Stay in of course!  Whether you have children or not, staying in and having a delicious home-cooked meal is a wonderful way to share an evening with someone you love.  Throw on some nice background music, light some candles and you're all set to enjoy a wonderful meal – just the two of you.

# Zesty Kale Salad

Kale is a leafy green vegetable that is being hailed as "the new beef", "the queen of greens" and "a nutritional powerhouse". Not only is it high in iron, calcium, Vitamin A, Vitamin C and fibre, it's has zero fat and is a great anti-inflammatory food!

Makes 4 cups

## Dressing:

- 2 ½ Tbsp freshly squeezed lemon juice
- 1 ½ Tbsp gluten free soy sauce (such as Bragg's)
- 2 ½ Tbsp water
- 1 garlic clove
- ½ tsp onion powder

## Salad:

- 3 ½ cups thinly sliced fresh kale
- ¼ cup red onion, chopped finely
- 1 cup thinly sliced English cucumber
- ½ red pepper, diced
- 3 Tbsp raw sunflower seeds

## Directions:

1. Combine dressing ingredients in a small jar with a lid and shake well. Set aside.
2. For the salad, combine the kale, onion, cucumber and red pepper in a salad bowl. Pour the dressing over the salad and toss well to combine.
3. Place in refrigerator for at least an hour. Just before serving, add the sunflower seeds, toss and serve.

# Garlic Bread

You're probably thinking – garlic on a romantic date?? Yes, I know it's not the most commonly used breath freshener but it tastes so good and is so good for you! If you're worried about the side-effects of garlic, just have some fresh mint handy. Pop a few leaves in your mouth or steep some into a warming cup of tea for a quick and natural breath freshener.

Makes 4 slices

## Ingredients:

- 4 slices Multigrain Loaf (See *Lunch with Friends* section) or other FRESH gluten free vegan bread
- 1 clove garlic, minced (or pressed through a garlic press)
- 2-3 Tbsp non-hydrogenated vegan margarine (such as Earth Balance)

1. Mix minced garlic and margarine together in a small bowl. Spread on each piece of bread and place on a cookie sheet.
2. Place under the broiler in oven and broil until brown and crunchy about 4-7 minutes. Watch carefully so the bread doesn't burn!

# Veggie Pasta Sauce

Lots of vegetables in a smooth tomato sauce make up this lovely topping to pasta. Pair it with any of the wonderful gluten-free pasta options that are on the market and you'll have quick and delicious meal that makes enough for leftovers – it even tastes better the next day!

Makes approximately 10 cups

## Ingredients:

- 1 package frozen spinach, thawed and excess water squeezed out
- 1 can or 2 cups of cooked chickpeas, drained and rinsed
- 2 -5.5 oz cans tomato paste mixed with enough water to make 4 cups
- 6 garlic cloves, minced
- 1 green pepper, chopped
- 1 can sliced mushrooms or 8 oz sliced fresh mushrooms
- 1 small zucchini, quartered and cut into ¼" pieces
- 1 ½ Tbsp Italian seasoning
- 1 ½ tsp dried basil
- 1-1 ½ tsp salt
- ¼ cup nutritional yeast flakes
- ½-1 tsp garlic powder
- ½-1 tsp onion powder
- ½ pound gluten free pasta of your choice

## Directions:

1. In a large pot, simmer garlic, peppers, zucchini and mushrooms in a little water to soften, usually a few minutes.

2. Add remaining ingredients (except pasta). Simmer for approximately 1 hour and serve over hot cooked pasta.

# {Special Notes}

- Sometimes it can be challenging to maintain a good texture without overcooking gluten free pasta. I've devised a method that's pretty foolproof for getting a nice final product. This should work for all shapes of pasta except spaghetti-style noodles. Simply bring a pot of water to a boil, add your noodles, stir and then cover the pot and turn off the heat. Let pasta sit in the hot water for 8-10 minutes. After this time, check and see if the noodles have reached desired doneness. If they have, drain and rinse with cold water to avoid any additional cooking. If they are still a little firm, let sit an additional 2-3 minutes, checking occasionally to see if they are done. Serve immediately.

# Sweetheart Brownies for Two

A take on my Peppermint Patty Brownie recipe, this simple yet delicious dessert is the perfect end to a romantic dinner for two.

## Ingredients:
## Brownie:

- 1/2 cup sugar
- 1/4 cup sorghum flour
- 1/4 cup brown rice flour
- 1/4 cup potato starch
- 1/2 cup carob powder
- 1/2 teaspoon baking powder
- 1/2 teaspoon xanthan gum
- 1/4 teaspoon salt
- 1/4 cup vegetable oil
- 1/2 cup soy or almond milk

## Cherry Topping:

- 1 cup fresh or frozen, thawed and drained pitted cherries, quartered (or halved if you like bigger pieces)
- 6 Tbsp water mixed with 1 Tbsp cornstarch
- ¼ cup maple syrup
- 2 tsp almond extract
- 1 tsp pure vanilla extract

## Toppings:

- Non-dairy whipped topping
- Fresh cherries for garnishing

## Directions:

1. Preheat oven to 350* F. Grease an 8" square pan or line with parchment paper.
2. In a medium bowl, mix together sugar, sorghum flour, rice flour, potato starch, carob powder, baking powder, xanthan gum and salt.
3. Add oil and non-dairy milk and stir well to combine. Pour into prepared pan and smooth.
4. Bake for 16-18 minutes or until brownie is slightly starting to pull away from the edges of the pan.  Cool completely.
5. To make the cherry topping, combine all of the topping ingredients in a saucepan.  With a whisk, stir over medium heat until thickened.  Cool completely.
6. Just before serving, cut the brownie into two large hearts using a heart cookie cutter.  If you don't have a heart cookie cutter, simply trace a heart onto a piece of cardboard or other stiff paper, place on top of brownie and cut around template.
7. Place each brownie on a plate, top with a generous scoop of cherry topping and a dollop of whipped topping. Garnish with a cherry and serve.

Notes:

*Notes:*

# Movie Night

Mexican Chili Corn Pie
Cheeze Sauce
Sunflower Sour Cream
Banana Splits
Banana Coconut Ice Cream

"Ah! There is nothing like staying at home, for real comfort."

Jane Austen

# Movie Night

I'll be honest – I'd rather have my wisdom teeth extracted than watch a movie! If you ask anyone who knows me, watching a movie is not anywhere on the top of my list of entertainment ideas. Now, watching a good, old fashioned TV show from the 1960's, a Pioneer history show, orchestral productions or anything that has to do with cooking or decorating cakes – *that* is something I'd sit down and enjoy. Whether you have a favorite show, movie or documentary that you love watching, it's always nice to have a night where you can sit down on your couch, turn on the tv and relax with some delicious food.

# Mexican Chili Corn Pie

This "one-pot" meal is one of our favorites!  I love it with avocadoes, salsa and *Sunflower Sour Cream* piled high on top!

Makes 6 servings

## Ingredients:

- 2 cloves garlic, minced
- 1 EACH red and green pepper, diced
- ½ cup diced celery
- 2 cups canned chopped tomatoes, drained slightly
- 1 ½ cups corn, canned or frozen
- 1 cup kidney, pinto or romano beans, drained and rinsed
- 1 can sliced black olives
- 2 tbsp onion powder
- ¼ cup nutritional yeast flakes
- 1 ½ tsp cumin
- 1 ½ tsp paprika
- 1/4 -1/2 tsp cayenne pepper
- Salt to taste

## Cornbread Topping

- ¾ cup cornmeal
- 1 tbsp brown rice flour
- ½ tsp salt
- 2 tsp baking powder
- 2 tbsp ground flax seed mixed with 4 Tbsp cold water, let sit for 10 minutes
- 6 tbsp non-dairy milk or water
- 1 tbsp olive oil
- ½ recipe Cheeze Sauce (see this section)

# $\mathcal{D}$irections:

1. In a large oven-proof skillet/frying pan, saute the garlic, peppers and celery in a small amount of water for 5-6 minutes until barely soft.
2. Stir in seasonings, tomatoes, corn and beans. Bring to a boil and simmer the mixture for 10 minutes.
3. Preheat oven to 425*F.
4. To make the cornbread, mix together cornmeal, rice flour, salt and baking powder. Combine the liquid ingredients separately and add to the dry mixture and stir until a smooth batter is formed.
5. Spoon over the mixture in the casserole dish. It will look like there's not much but It will rise and expand when baking. Spread Cheeze Sauce on top (you may not need the whole amount) and bake for 25-30 minutes or until cornbread is golden and firm.
6. Serve hot with avocado slices, salsa and Sunflower Sour Cream.

# {$\mathcal{S}pecial\ \mathcal{N}otes$}

- A special thank-you to the Lifestyle Matters Team for allowing me to pass along some of their wonderful recipes. For more information or for other recipes, please visit www.lifestylematters.com

# Cheeze Sauce

This creamy cheese-style sauce is a wonderful topping to steamed vegetables, potatoes or our favorite – Haystacks!  The jalapeno pepper is optional but it really does make this sauce extra nice.

Makes 3 cups

## Ingredients:
- ¼ cup unsalted cashews
- 2 ½ cups water
- ½ Tbsp lemon juice
- ½ red pepper, seeded and chopped coarsely
- ½ medium jalapeno pepper (approximately a 1 ½" piece), seeds removed, optional OR heaping 1/8 tsp jalapeno powder
- ¼-1/3 cup nutritional yeast flakes
- 1 tsp onion powder
- 1/3 tsp garlic powder
- ¼ cup brown rice flour
- 1 tsp salt or to taste

## Directions:
1. Blend all ingredients with 1 1/2 cups water in a blender until smooth.
2. Pour into saucepan and add remaining 1 cup water to the blender.  Blend briefly for a few seconds.  This "cleans" the blender out so as not to leave any of the delicious sauce behind!
3. Heat over medium heat, stirring often with a whisk until thick.
4. Serve hot.  Keeps well for several days in refrigerator and reheats easily.

# {Special Notes}

- Be sure to check the ingredients when buying cashews or other nuts. Choose nuts that are either raw or roasted and unsalted. Dry roasted nuts quite often contain wheat so make sure you read the ingredient list carefully.
- When cutting and removing seeds from jalapenos, it's best to wear gloves as the oils in the peppers can really irritate your skin. A melon baller works great at quickly extracting the seeds and veins from the pepper. Remember to remove your gloves carefully when done and do not touch your eyes, nose or mouth!

# Sunflower Sour Cream

While this doesn't taste identical to traditional sour cream, it makes for a great topping on baked potatoes and goes well with Potato Skins.

Makes approximately 1 ½ cups

## Ingredients:

- 1 cup raw sunflower seeds
- 1 ¼ + 2 Tbsp cup water
- ¾ tsp salt
- ¾ tsp onion powder
- ¾ tsp garlic powder
- 3-4 Tbsp lemon juice

## Directions:

1. Place all ingredients in a blender and blend until smooth. This will thicken up as it chills.

# Banana Splits

Healthy Banana Splits?  You bet!  Refined sugar free, full of fruit and delicious describe this dessert that's sure to be a winner with both adults and children.

Makes 5 banana splits

## Ingredients:

- 5 ripe bananas
- 1 recipe Banana Coconut Ice Cream – see recipe in this section
- 1 small can crushed pineapple, drained
- 1 small jar naturally sweetened (preferably) strawberry jam
- Gluten Free Sprinkles, optional
- Cherries for garnish, optional
- Non-dairy whipped topping, optional

## Directions:

1. Ahead of time, prepare Carob Fudge Sauce and Honey-Sweetened Strawberry jam according to recipe directions.
2. Approximately 20-30 minutes before you are ready to serve your dessert, make the Banana Coconut Ice Cream according to the recipe directions.
3. Once ice cream has reached desired thickness, start assembling your Banana Splits.  Split a banana lengthwise, place in a banana split boat or other boat and add ice cream.
4. Top with remaining toppings and serve.

# Banana Coconut Ice Cream

This can be served alone or made into Banana Splits for a delicious ending to a meal.

Makes 4-5 servings

## Ingredients:

- 1-400 mL can full-fat coconut cream
- 3-4 bananas, peeled, cut in chunks and frozen for several hours or overnight
- 1 tsp coconut extract
- 1 tsp pure vanilla extract

## Directions:

1. Beforehand, peel and cut bananas into ½ inch chunks. Freeze until solid for a few hours or overnight.
2. Place all ingredients into a blender and blend until smooth. Pour into frozen ice cream maker drum and churn for 15-20 minutes or until desired consistency.

## {Special Notes}

- Using bananas that are as ripe as possible will give you a sweeter ice cream. If you prefer your ice cream a little sweeter, add some honey or maple syrup to the blender just before mixing.
- If you don't have an ice cream maker, you can still whip up this delicious treat. Just use the food processor and make sure all your ingredients are thoroughly chilled beforehand. The finished product won't be quite the same but it will still be delicious nonetheless!

# *Seasonings and Extras*

Parmesan Cheeze Please!
Curry Powder Substitute
Chicken-style Seasoning
Measuring Equivalents
List of beans
Bean Cooking Chart – Regular or
Pressure Cooker method
Dried bean quick-soak method
Pantry Checklist
Resources

# Parmesan Cheeze Please!

This is a great substitute for Parmesan Cheese. It goes perfectly on spaghetti and in Caesar salad dressing. Experiment and use it on other things as well and you'll be pleasantly surprised!

## Ingredients:

- 1 cup sesame seeds
- 1/3 cup nutritional yeast flakes
- 2 tsp onion powder
- 1 tsp garlic powder
- 1 tsp salt

## Directions:

1. Place all ingredients into a bowl and mix thoroughly. Place half of the mixture into an electric coffee mill and grind well. Repeat with the remaining ingredients.
2. Freezes well.

# Curry Powder Substitute

Curry powder is simply a mixture of various spices and is usually quite hot. This curry powder is much milder but still gives a great curry flavor.

## Ingredients:

- 1 Tbsp coriander
- 2 tsp cumin
- 2 Tbsp celery seed
- 1 tsp garlic powder
- 1 1/2 Tbsp turmeric
- ½ tsp cardamom
- 1 Tbsp onion powder

## Directions:

1. Mix all ingredients together in a bowl. Store in a glass jar or airtight container.

# Chicken-Style Seasoning

I use this seasoning to replace traditional chicken seasoning and chicken stock in recipes. It can be used in a variety of ways including adding flavor to soups, rice, beans – anything! You can typically make your own broth by using 1 Tbsp seasoning in 2-2 ½ cups water.

## Ingredients:

- 3 Tbsp sea salt
- ½ cup nutritional yeast flakes
- ½ tsp turmeric
- ½ tsp marjoram
- 1 ¼ tsp garlic powder
- ¼ tsp sage
- ¼ tsp summer or winter savory
- 1 Tbsp onion powder
- 1 Tbsp dried parsley

## Directions:

1. Place all ingredients into blender or grinder. Blend thoroughly and store in a glass mason jar, either in the refrigerator or in a cool, dark place like a pantry.

## {Special Notes}

- Thank you to LifeStyle Matters for allowing me to use this great recipe! www.lifestylematters.com

# Measuring Equivalents

1 Tablespoon = 3 teaspoons

1/8 cup = 2 Tablespooons

¼ cup = 4 Tablespoons

1/3 cup = 5 Tablespoons + 1 teaspoon

½ cup = 8 Tablespoons

2/3 cup = 10 Tablespoons + 2 teaspoons

¾ cup = 12 Tablespoons

1 cup = 48 teaspoons

1 cup = 16 Tablespoons

8 fluid ounces = 1 cup

1 pint – 2 cups

1 quart = 2 pints

4 cups = 1 quart

1 gallon = 4 quarts

16 ounces = 1 pound

# Dried Beans and Legumes

When it comes to dried beans, peas and lentils, there is a rainbow of options out there!  Some require soaking while others don't so please refer to my chart on the next page that takes the guesswork out of cooking beans.

- Chick peas
- Lentils – green, red, french, black beluga and more!
- Black beans
- Pinto beans
- Romano beans
- Black eyed peas
- Yellow eyed beans
- Navy beans
- Fava beans
- Lima beans
- Soy beans – including tofu and tempeh
- Split peas – green and yellow
- Hundreds of other varieties if you grow them yourself

# Bean Cooking Chart — Regular & Pressure Cooker Methods

| Dried Beans (1 cup) | Soaking Time | Regular Cooking Time | Pressure Cook Time |
|---|---|---|---|
| Adzuki | none | 45-50 minutes | 15-20 minutes |
| Black (Turtle) | overnight | 45-60 minutes | 15-20 minutes |
| Black-Eyed Peas | overnight | 1 hour | 10 minutes |
| Chick Peas | overnight | 1 ½-2 ½ hours | 20 minutes |
| Kidney | overnight | 1 – 1 ½ hours | 10 minutes |
| Lentil – Red | none | 20-30 minutes | 5-7 minutes |
| Lentil – Green | none | 30-45 minutes | 6-8 minutes |
| Lima | overnight | 60-90 minutes | not recommended |
| Lima, Baby | overnight | 45-50 minutes | not recommended |
| Mung | overnight | 1 – 1 ½ hours | 8-10 minutes |
| Pea, split | none | 35-40 minutes | not recommend |
| Pinto | overnight | 1 ½ hours | 10 minutes |
| Soybean | overnight | 3 hours | 15 minutes |
| White (Navy) | overnight | 45-60 minutes | 10 minutes |

# Bean Quick-Soaking Method:

Beans are a great source of fibre and protein but they contain high levels of phytic acid which is an enzyme inhibitor as well as a binder to important minerals such as copper, zinc, calcium, magnesium, and iron and can potentially lead to a deficiency. But there are ways to drastically decrease the amount of phytic acid in beans and that is by soaking them or sprouting them.

Whether you're soaking the beans overnight or using my Quick Soak method below, including this important step in your bean preparation will help you to eliminate much of this mineral-binding substance. {Please note – if you choose to soak your beans overnight, it's best to place them in the refrigerator while soaking. This helps to reduce the risk of growth from any bacteria that may be present.}

This Quick Soak method is used in place of soaking beans overnight.

1  Pour desired amount of beans into pot. Cover with water, making sure water level is at least 2-3 inches higher than the amount of beans in your pot.
2  Bring to a boil and boil beans for 2 minutes. Cover, turn off heat, and leave to soak for 2 hours.

3 Once the beans are finished soaking, drain, rinse and cook using the preferred method (either boiling water or pressure cooker) as laid out in the Bean Cooking Chart.

# Pantry Check List

These are some of the items that I try to have on hand all the time. I haven't included a whole lot of fresh produce because I know it can be hard to always have fresh items on hand. Also, everyone has their own tastes for fresh produce so add in what you and your family prefer.

- ✓ Almonds, raw
- ✓ Apple juice concentrate, frozen
- ✓ Apples
- ✓ Applesauce, unsweetened
- ✓ Bananas
- ✓ Brown Rice - Short Grain, Long Grain or Basmati
- ✓ Canned peaches
- ✓ Canned tomatoes
- ✓ Canned, sliced black olives
- ✓ Carob chips (gluten free – not barley malt sweetened)
- ✓ Carob powder
- ✓ Carrots
- ✓ Cashews, raw and unsalted
- ✓ Celery
- ✓ Chicken-style seasoning
- ✓ Coconut milk and coconut cream
- ✓ Coconut oil
- ✓ Cold pressed, extra virgin olive oil

- ✓ Dried beans – our favorites are pinto beans, kidney beans, yellow-eyed beans and chick peas
- ✓ Dried herbs and seasonings such as basil, oregano, garlic powder, onion powder, sea salt, dried parsley, paprika, turmeric, thyme, sage, summer savory, dill weed and marjoram
- ✓ Flax seeds
- ✓ Frozen corn
- ✓ Frozen fruit such as bananas, strawberries, blueberries or blackberries (these can be easily added to smoothies or crisps)
- ✓ Frozen mixed vegetables
- ✓ Frozen peas
- ✓ Frozen chopped red peppers (for Cheeze Sauce and stir fries)
- ✓ Garlic
- ✓ Gluten free corn chips
- ✓ Gluten free flours – our favorites are brown rice flour, potato starch, potato flour, sorghum flour, buckwheat flour and tapioca starch/flour
- ✓ Gluten free soy sauce
- ✓ Greens such as spinach, kale or swiss chard (fresh or frozen – either way, it can be added to smoothies and scrambled tofu easily)
- ✓ Honey
- ✓ Instant Tapioca
- ✓ Lemon juice

- ✓ Lentils – French, green and red are the most commonly used
- ✓ Maple syrup
- ✓ Nutritional yeast, flaked
- ✓ Onions
- ✓ Orange juice concentrate, frozen
- ✓ Peanut butter or other nut butters
- ✓ Potatoes
- ✓ Premade gluten free flour blend
- ✓ Pumpkin seeds
- ✓ Quinoa
- ✓ Raisins
- ✓ Split peas
- ✓ Sprouts and sprouting seeds
- ✓ Stevia
- ✓ Sunflower seeds, raw and unsalted
- ✓ Tahini
- ✓ Tofu – Firm, Extra Firm and Silken
- ✓ Tomato paste
- ✓ Unsweetened coconut
- ✓ Vanilla extract, pure
- ✓ Walnuts and/or pecans
- ✓ Wheat free oats
- ✓ Xanthan gum

# Resources:

Below is a list of various health-related and gluten-free-friendly resources, books, restaurants and websites that I have found helpful:

- Ministry of Healing
  - Excellent book written on the subject of health and wellness
- Counsels on Diet and Foods
  - Another great book outlining good health as it pertains to our food/dietary habits
- www.lifestylematters.com
  - Great site that includes some recipes, cookbooks and healthy living tips
- www.amazingfacts.org
  - Huge archive of articles, videos and audio programs, many dealing with health-related topics
  - They also have an online bookstore which sells several vegetarian/vegan cookbooks
- Adventist Book Centre
  - Online or visit their store in Oshawa, Ontario. www.adventistbookcentre.com. They also have a mobile store that visits various cities. Call for current bookmobile schedule.
- www.bibleuniverse.com
  - Free online Bible school – or choose to have the free lessons sent to you via the mail. Topics on health are covered.
- http://www.theveggieliciousdietitian.blogspot.ca
  - Bev Miller's blog – full of great healthy living information!
- Wildwood Lifestyle Program
  - http://www.wildwoodhealth.org/lifestyle/
  - Offers health services and 11 or 25 day Lifestyle Programs for anyone seeking to improve their health
- Centurion Ministries
  - Medical Missionary site with information on healthy living

- www.rawnutrition.ca
  - Online source for sprouting seeds, small kitchen appliances such as dehydrators, juicers, sprouters, etc., and a large selection of health resources. Canadian-owned and operated and based out of Otter Lake, Quebec
- www.celiac.ca
  - Canadian Celiac Association
  - Great website with a lot of information for anyone following a gluten free diet
  - Several books are available including an "Acceptability of Foods and Food Ingredients for the Gluten-Free Diet" Pocket Dictionary. This great little book fits into a purse or pocket and is handy when you're in a situation where you're unsure about the safety of certain ingredients
- www.csaceliacs.info/grains_and_flours_glossary.jsp
  - Celiac Sprue Association
  - Grains and flours glossary – large list of flours/grains that are labelled as:
    1. Consistent with a gluten free diet at this time
    2. Questionable due to content, contact or contamination
    3. Not consistent with a gluten free diet at this time
- The Mix Company – www.themixcompany.com
  - This is a great gluten free business out of Eganville, Ontario. It is owned and operated by Randy and Cate Ott who have been in the business for years. They offer a wide selection of gluten free mixes including bread, muffins, cookies, seasoning packets and much more. Many of their mixes are vegetarian/vegan and most can be made that way with a few substitutions.
- Kasha Natural Foods, Pembroke
  - Health food store with lots of options. Offers many gluten free and vegetarian/vegan products.
- Integrated Nutrition, Pembroke

- o Nutrition store with many items to choose from
- Baker Creek Seeds –www.rareseeds.com
  - o Excellent heirloom seed company; offers 1400 varieties of seeds for you to grow your own healthy and delicious heirloom vegetables and plants
- Purest, Perth, Ontario (and in many retail locations)
  - o Non-GMO, Kosher, no artificial ingredients
  - o Offers gluten free flours, mixes, and more (excellent source for gluten free millet flour)
  - o Their retail location in Perth also offers bulk gluten free flour options
- The Green Earth Restaurant, Ottawa (100% vegan but not strictly gluten free so be sure to notify your server of any allergies that you have)
- The Green Door Restaurant, Ottawa – gluten free and vegan options are labelled
- The Table Restaurant, Ottawa – buffet style; gluten free and vegan options are clearly marked
- Tea Tree Restaurant, Toronto – all vegetarian with some vegan and gluten free options
- Le Commensal, Toronto – all vegetarian with some vegan and gluten free options
- Crudessence – Montreal – raw and vegan restaurant
- The Magic Oven, Toronto – gluten free and vegan pizza available
- Kelly's Bake Shoppe, Burlington – all vegan and all gluten free
- KindFood, Burlington – all vegan and all gluten free
- The Naked Sprout, Burlington – all vegan, all gluten free and some raw
- Rawlicious, Barrie and Toronto – all vegan, all gluten free and all raw

# $\mathcal{I}ndex$

5 Common Gluten Free Mistakes .................................................................. 14

About this book ........................................................................................ 11

Author's Note .......................................................................................... 9

Avocado Key Lime Pie ............................................................................ 123

Baked Rice Loaf ..................................................................................... 56

Banana Blueberry Pancakes .................................................................. 138

Banana Coconut Ice Cream ................................................................... 190

Banana Splits ........................................................................................ 189

Barbecue Sauce .................................................................................... 116

Bean Cooking Chart .............................................................................. 199

Black Bean Burgers .............................................................................. 120

Blueberry Cream Trifle .......................................................................... 108

Blueberry Muffins (with variations) ........................................................ 130

Braised Peas ......................................................................................... 55

Brownies, Peppermint Patty ................................................................. 152

Burgers, Black Bean ............................................................................. 120

Cheesecake with Raspberry Sauce ....................................................... 60

Cheeze Sauce ....................................................................................... 186

Cherry Fudgesicles or Ice Cream .......................................................... 76

Chick Pea Tuna Salad ........................................................................... 100

Chicken-style Seasoning ....................................................................... 196

Cookies, Thumbprint ............................................................................. 48

Crackers, Rosemary Corn Crackers ....................................................... 40

Cranberry Banana Muffins .................................................................... 132

Cream of Cauliflower Soup .................................................................... 158

Creamy Garlic Spread ........................................................................... 122

Creamy Pasta Bake .............................................................................. 68

Cupcakes, Orange Delight ..................................................................... 74

Curried Pumpkin Soup .......................................................................... 160

Curried Rice Salad ................................................................................ 106

Curried Zucchini Hummus .................................................................. 42
Curry Powder Substitute ................................................................ 195
Dedication ..........................................................................................7
Dip, Hot Broccoli & Mushroom .................................................... 148
Dried bean quick-soak method ................................................... 200
Eggless "Egg" Salad ........................................................................ 99
Fruit Kebabs ................................................................................... 136
Garlic Baked Squash ........................................................................ 54
Garlic Bread ................................................................................... 173
Gluten Free Flours ........................................................................... 13
Gravy, Mushroom ............................................................................ 58
Green Bean Casserole ...................................................................... 86
Guacamole ..................................................................................... 147
Hidden Sources of Gluten ............................................................... 20
Hot Broccoli & Mushroom Dip ..................................................... 148
Hummus ......................................................................................... 101
Hummus, Curried Zucchini .............................................................. 42
Ice Cream, Banana Coconut ......................................................... 190
Lemony Dill Pickles ....................................................................... 119
Lentil Salad .................................................................................... 105
Lettuce Wraps .................................................................................. 98
List of beans ................................................................................... 198
Maple Pecan Tarts ........................................................................... 91
Mashed Potatoes Supreme .............................................................. 57
Measuring Equivalents .................................................................. 197
Mexican Chili Corn Pie ................................................................. 184
Mexican Pie ................................................................................... 150
Mini Pizzas ....................................................................................... 70
Muffins, Blueberry (with variations) ............................................ 130
Muffins, Cranberry Banana ........................................................... 132
Multigrain Loaf .............................................................................. 164
Mushroom Gravy ............................................................................. 58
Oatmeal Raisin Scones .................................................................. 134

Orange Delight Cupcakes .................................................................... 74
Orange Strawberry Banana Smoothie ............................................. 137
Pantry Checklist ................................................................................. 202
Parmesan Cheeze Please! ................................................................ 194
Pasta, Creamy Bake .......................................................................... 68
Pasta, Salsa Skillet ............................................................................ 118
Peas, Braised ...................................................................................... 55
Peppermint Patty Brownies .............................................................. 152
Perfect Pie Crust................................................................................. 46
Pickles, Lemony Dill........................................................................... 119
Pie Crust, Perfect............................................................................... 46
Pizza Popcorn ................................................................................... 146
Pizza Sauce ........................................................................................ 72
Popcorn, Pizza ................................................................................... 146
Popsicles, Yogurt Yum-Yum............................................................... 73
Potato Salad....................................................................................... 117
Potato Skins ........................................................................................ 144
Potatoes, Mashed Supreme ............................................................. 57
Quiche................................................................................................. 43
Quinoa Tabbouleh ............................................................................ 44
Relish, Zucchini .................................................................................. 102
Resources............................................................................................ 206
Rice Loaf, Baked................................................................................ 56
Roasted Root Vegetables ................................................................ 84
Rosemary Corn Crackers.................................................................. 40
Salad, Chick Pea Tuna...................................................................... 100
Salad, Curried Rice............................................................................ 106
Salad, Eggless "Egg" ......................................................................... 99
Salad, Summer Tomato ..................................................................... 104
Salad, Veggie Taco........................................................................... 162
Salsa Skillet Pasta .............................................................................. 118
Sauteed Greens.................................................................................. 85
Savory Baked Tofu ............................................................................ 90

Scones, Oatmeal Raisin ..................................................................134
Seasonings and Extras ..................................................................193
Smoothie, Orange Strawberry Banana .......................................137
Soup, Cream of Cauliflower ..........................................................158
Soup, Curried Pumpkin ..................................................................160
Sour Cream, Sunflower ..................................................................188
Squash, Garlic Baked ......................................................................54
Stamppot Carrots .............................................................................82
Strawberry Macaroon Bars ...........................................................166
Stuffing ..............................................................................................88
Summer Tomato Salad ...................................................................104
Sunflower Sour Cream ...................................................................188
Sweetheart Brownies for Two .......................................................176
Tabbouleh, Quinoa..........................................................................44
Tarts, Maple Pecan ..........................................................................91
Thumbprint Cookies .........................................................................48
Tips for Gluten Free Success ...........................................................22
Tips to get you started on a Plant-based diet .............................33
Tofu, Savory Baked ..........................................................................90
Trifle, Blueberry Cream ..................................................................108
Veggie Pasta Sauce ......................................................................174
Veggie Taco Salad .........................................................................162
What is Gluten? ................................................................................12
Where are you getting your Fibre? ................................................25
Why Vegan/Vegetarian? ................................................................30
Yogurt Yum-Yum Popsicles ..............................................................73
Zesty Kale Salad ............................................................................172
Zucchini Relish................................................................................102

Made in the USA
Charleston, SC
03 November 2013